T0008187

Praise for I Quit

"I've said it a thousand times. So have you: *I'm going to take care of myself*. Smith actually does it, with clarity, humor, and deep interrogation into the societal complexities and personal histories of alcohol, weed, caffeine, food, and social media—the things that save us and, at the same time, drain us dry. *I Quit Everything* doesn't ask *us* to quit; it asks us to pay attention, to listen to our bodies, to find what serves us and hold on like the holy goddamn grail. I loved it." —**Megan Stielstra, author of *The Wrong Way to Save Your Life***

"Smith is such an engaging, probing writer that you're hanging on tight for this brisk ride, as each question begets a bigger question that she investigates as well as lives. . . . The one thing you can't quit is reading *I Quit Everything*." —**Mark Caro, author of *The Foie Gras Wars* and host of the *Caropop* podcast**

"A classic example of addition by subtraction, *I Quit Everything* provides an abundance of helpful advice—and hope—to anyone feeling stuck in their ways and looking for a change."
—**Annie Zaleski, author of a 33 1/3 book on Duran Duran's *Rio*, and illustrated biographies of Lady Gaga and Pink**

"Reading *I Quit Everything* is like having a heart-to-heart with your smartest friend—cups of spearmint tea steaming as the conversation goes from personal disclosure to pop-culture analysis to philosophical inquiry and back. Freda Love Smith writes at one point that this is an 'anti-self-help' book, and it does offer much more than your average bullet-pointed guide past a midlife crisis. But it helped me, because as a sometimes impulsive, often self-critical, always curious woman at midlife, I related so much to Smith's desire to both reset her life and celebrate all she's lived through. Heartening and challenging." —**Ann Powers, author of** *Good Booty: Love and Sex, Black and White, Body and Soul in American Music*

Praise for Red Velvet Underground:
A Rock Memoir, with Recipes

"These are sweet, unsentimental scenes from the ever-evolving life of a woman of many shifting and balancing roles: mother, wife, drummer, student, teacher, friend, daughter, food enthusiast. It's all tied together with tantalizing recipes that have been lovingly improvised and tweaked into a life-affirming doneness." —**Juliana Hatfield, musician**

"*Red Velvet Underground* is not only a rock memoir and recipe book but also a poignant work of personal self-discovery and the challenges yet joys of parenting." —**David Chiu,** *Huffington Post*

"This memoir is filled with twists and turns, rises and falls—all chronicled with Freda's characteristic charm and seductive wit. You might call it *Eat, Play, Love.* . . a wealth of road stories and recipes to share." —**Anthony DeCurtis, contributing editor at** *Rolling Stone*

"Thoughtful and wry, [Smith]'s a storyteller who doesn't scrub out blemishes but reminds readers just how much being an individual still matters, even in adulthood." —**Mark Guarino,** *Chicago Tribune*

I Quit Everything

How One Woman's Addiction to Quitting Helped Her Confront Bad Habits and Embrace Midlife

Freda Love Smith

MIDWAY

AGATE

CHICAGO

The events expressed in this book, while true, were composed from the author's memory. Some of the names and identities of people in this book have been altered or composited for the sake of simplicity and to protect privacy.

The information provided in this book should not be used for diagnosing or treating a health problem or disease. It is not a substitute for professional care. If you have or suspect you may have a health problem, you should consult your health care provider.

Lyrics from "Changed the Locks" have been reprinted by permission from Lucinda Williams.

First printed in September 2023

Printed in the United States of America

10 9 8 7 6 5 4 3 2 1   23 24 25 26 27

Library of Congress Cataloging-in-Publication Data
Names: Smith, Freda Love, author.
Title: I quit everything : how I survived the pandemic, tackled anxiety,
and confronted midlife through the power of quitting / Freda Love Smith.
Description: Chicago : Midway, [2023]Identifiers: LCCN 2023007818 (print) | LCCN
2023007819 (ebook) | ISBN
9781572843271 (paperback) | ISBN 9781572848771 (ebook)
Subjects: LCSH: Substance abuse. | Social media addiction. | Self-help
techniques.
Classification: LCC HV4998 .S62 2023 (print) | LCC HV4998 (ebook) | DDC
362.29--dc23/eng/20230513
LC record available at https://lccn.loc.gov/2023007818
LC ebook record available at https://lccn.loc.gov/2023007819

Cover design by Morgan Krehbiel
Author photo by Alex Hazel

Midway is an imprint of Agate Publishing. Agate books are available in bulk at discount prices. For more information, visit agatepublishing.com.

For Faith

"This quitting thing, it's a hard habit to break once you start."

Coach Morris Buttermaker

The Bad News Bears

Contents

I Quit

What Condition My Condition Was In

January 2021, TEN months into the Era of Covid, I was not tip-top: twenty pounds above fighting weight, blood pressure high, heart erratic and running away from me, stopping and starting, an overstressed engine. My sleep was fitful, sweaty. I frequently wondered: Is this a heart attack? Do I need an ambulance? Like everyone, I was anxious. Vaccines not yet widely available, more than three thousand people dying of Covid daily, and the hospitals overflowing. There was no room for me. I would be fine. On the surface, I looked fine—a reasonably healthy fifty-three-year-old, mostly vegetarian, who practiced yoga and meditation.

I wasn't fine. Working from home at my university job as an academic advisor and lecturer kept me sedentary: no more walking to and from campus, no more running over to the student union for a snack break, no more stomping into downtown Evanston for lunch. I was growing sluggish, and compensated for this by slamming cup after cup of strong black tea while staring into my laptop screen for hours a day, advising students whose affects ranged from flat to furious to bereaved—this wasn't what college was meant to be. *How am I supposed to get a job in the film industry*, snapped one, *if I don't learn how to operate a camera?* To him, I personified all of it: the pandemic, the lockdown, the overnight switch to remote learning, the evaporation of social life and creative life, and his wavering hope for the future. In my ten years on the job, I had usually managed to answer my advisees' questions. My eyes stung. *We'll figure it out, somehow*, was my lame reply.

I could relate. My creative outlets had dried up, too. I had been a busy rock drummer before March 2020, playing regularly with my Chicago band Sunshine Boys, and that had ground to a full stop. My family and social life similarly contracted: Thanksgiving consisted of a family Zoom and a Tupperware container full of stuffed kabocha squash and roasted brussels sprouts that I passed to my youngest son in front of my apartment building for him to take home and reheat alone. Christmas was another Zoom and a wintery walk. In the absence of a social life, I loitered on Facebook and Instagram, ensnared by the absurd hope that I would find solace. At night, I sought relief in cannabis gummies and Scotch whisky. In the morning, I cleared the fog with stronger tea. I grew fatter, sadder, more anxious, my heart racing, like it thought it could run away from me and find a better home. I sweated through multiple shirts in my sleep, peeling them off, dropping them bedside, awakening to a damp, acrid pile. It felt like someone else's mess. *My* body had done that? I pulled on a clean, dry shirt, slipped a headband over my neglected, frizzy hair, clicked on the "pretty filter" on Zoom, and met with students. I kept my pajama bottoms on. I looked fine.

How's That Dry January Going?

It was January 6 and between Zoom meetings and appointments I sat paralyzed at my desk, watching glass shatter and a confederate flag wave. I saw someone we'd later know as Q Shaman, his face painted red, white, and blue, his head adorned with bearskin and horns, wielding a spear, striding gleefully through the U.S. Capitol, around him a swarm of punching, chanting, bloodthirsty rebels, searching for Speaker of the House Nancy Pelosi and Vice President Mike Pence. There was a noose. All of them following the direct order of the actual president of the United States.

Seven people died. One hundred fifty police officers were injured. Hundreds of workers were traumatized.

How's that dry January going? tweeted writer Rebecca Makkai.

In 2020, over a quarter of Americans drank more booze than they ever had before. Sales of premixed cocktails skyrocketed; online alcohol sales increased 262 percent; binge drinking in women increased 41 percent.[1] We were stuck at home, sad, worried, and lonely. Studies show that light or moderate drinkers are happier and mentally healthier than teetotalers, but the presence of others—drinking buddies—appears to be key to this happiness. Drinking socially can make us joyful, even ecstatic, but drinking alone tends to leave us even more depressed than we were before. Kate Julian, writing for *The Atlantic*, describes this kind of drinking as the "can't-bear-another-day-like-all-the-other-days variety." We weren't drinking to feel good. We were drinking to "take the edge off of feeling bad."[2]

I was partaking in this exact flavor of sad drinking. As I'd headed into winter break a month earlier, I knew I was likely to heavily imbibe (I'd been turning to the bottle even harder since the November 2020 election) and I tried an experiment: I ordered a case of fancy, herbal nonalcoholic cocktails, enticing alternatives to a glass of whiskey. But on the second night of break I poured one of those bottles—an infusion of dark cherry, chocolate, and elderberry—over ice, took a sip, and decided that it would be even better with a shot of whiskey. Another night, another booze-free cocktail, and . . . this one wanted vodka.

And on January 6? There wasn't enough booze in the world.

That night I couldn't sleep, even after three shots and a 10 milligram cannabis gummy. The words "dry" and "January" spiraled in my stoned head. What did it mean to be dry? How was it even possible? And what was January? Had 2020 actually ended? Had 2021 actually begun? And would we survive to see it end? The words melded into one: Dryjanuary. Drigeannuary.

Inaugurate

I WAS A full-time advisor in the School of Communication at Northwestern University, working with students in the Department of Radio/Television/Film, and for an entire decade I'd attended a Wednesday morning meeting with my advisor colleagues. On Wednesday, January 20, 2021, the undergraduate dean posted on Teams that she was cancelling our meeting so we could watch the inauguration. We never cancelled that meeting. It was the right call. *We need this*, someone wrote.

I turned off my computer and moved to the living room with a cup of tea. My husband, Jake, a professor at Northwestern, was working from home too and we sat together in anxious silence. It felt like we'd each sucked a long breath in and held it suspended. The ceremony began; there were pauses, lapses, stretches of time where nothing happened, long, long waits. The longest silence was before Biden's swearing in. It stretched for a million years, and in that expanse of time my heart lurched like a malfunctioning metronome. Jake and I exhaled a stream of exclamations. *What's wrong?* I said. *What the hell is happening?* said

Jake. I dug my chewed-up fingernails into the arms of my chair.

The proceedings proceeded. No shots rang, no buildings or bodies fell. But something in me snapped. *I need a fucking drink*, I said. *I need a fucking drink right now.* I meant it more than ever I had. It was noon on Wednesday. I'd scheduled student advising appointments on Zoom that afternoon. All I wanted was to get blotto. Would it help? Were all these drinks I'd had, every night, night after night—were they making anything better or just pushing me deeper into a hole? *For there is always light*, said Amanda Gorman, fresh-faced and brilliant, *if only we're brave enough to see it.*

The only thing I felt brave enough for was a stiff drink. That desperate desire for a noontime whiskey triggered an inner rupture. I saw myself: sad, exhausted, desperate for escape after a year of pandemic and four years of Trump. I'd been gradually falling apart and now the process seemed complete. *I have to stop*, I thought. *I have to quit.* Not forever. For a while. That night I drank a cup of chamomile tea and climbed into bed early. Still, I couldn't sleep. It was too hot in the bedroom. I aggressively kicked off the blankets. Soon I was freezing and I hauled them back in place. I flopped left to right. Jake bailed for the guest room. *Dryjanuary*, I thought. What's the impetus for all those people to give up drink at the start of the year? A reset, a kind of fast, a detox. I needed a big reset, more than a month could offer. Six months, I decided, minimum. A dry half year. Instead of continuing to booze my way through the brutal Covid winter, I would try to take it straight.

All of Me

THE MORNING AFTER, my resolve hadn't wavered. I cooked a virtuous breakfast, oatmeal and fruit and nuts, signifying my determination for self-improvement. I ate slowly, thinking things through. I was really going to do this. But was it enough to just quit booze? What about my other bad habits and addictions? I was overconsuming caffeine, too; in fact I was a full-on tea junky. My crazy heartbeats were starting to freak me out, and all that caffeine was surely making things worse. I was eating too much sugar, exacerbating my nighttime sweats and contributing to the weight gain. I ate a high-dose cannabis edible every night, and if I wasn't exactly addicted, I was certainly dependent. And long hours on social media had become an exhausting habit with an icky, compulsive quality.

By the end of that bowl of oatmeal, I'd decided: I had to quit everything. All of it.

I would drop one addiction a month. In January I'd quit booze, in February I'd quit sugar, in March—cannabis, in April, caffeine, and in May I'd abandon all social media. In June, July, and

August I'd stay off everything and see what it felt like to be free.

We had all been forced to quit so much. We quit gathering for holidays and birthdays, quit seeing or playing live music, quit going to movies, quit hugging our parents, quit having lunch with our coworkers, quit visiting our friends, quit singing in church. And here I was, quitting by choice the very coping practices that I'd turned to in the face of those constraints. Why not take all of me? After I stripped away these habits and addictions, what would remain? It scared me to think about all the parts of myself I would lose by quitting; it scared me more to think about the parts of myself I might find.

Alcohol

I Drink Not, Therefore I Am Not

I HAD A drinking problem in my late teens and early twenties and subsequently spent a couple of years in strict sobriety, firmly convinced that I could not and would not ever drink again. Now here I was, thirty years later, quitting again.

Giving up booze this time was less difficult physically, but it was harder emotionally, for two reasons. First, the removal of comfort and relief, that sweet numbness yanked away. There was nothing to soften the discomfort of the bleak winter, the relentlessly terrible news, the exhausting stress of uncertainty. I was an exposed nerve. The second thing was much more confusing: drinking had become intimately integrated into my selfhood. When I was younger, a bandmate had nicknamed me—partly affectionately, partly meanly—"Freda Lush" (a twist on "Freda Love"), and I never minded, I kind of liked it. Recently, a close friend gave me a gorgeous cocktail cookbook for Christmas. This was the kind of gift someone who knew me well would give me. I wasn't sure who I was without booze, or if I even existed without. How had drinking become one of my essential traits? I turned intuitively to movies for an answer, searching for clues by revisiting my childhood and young adult favorites, movies that had imprinted on me, shaped me, pointed me towards my future. What I found is that my young self had been magnetically drawn to stories of unrepentant souses.

I'm Loose

I DREW UP a list of movies about drunks. The first was *The Bad News Bears* (1976), starring Walter Matthau as Morris Buttermaker, a washed-up baseball player turned pool cleaner, hired to coach a team of misfit Little Leaguers. It's a movie about the toxicity of competition, power and exclusion and inclusion, childhood and adulthood and sadness and love.

And beer. It's very much a movie about beer.

The movie opens with Buttermaker's convertible slamming to a stop in the lawn by a Little League baseball field. He pulls a beer from the cooler, dumps some out, and adds a generous topper of whiskey. The movie closes with a pile of triumphant ten- and eleven-year-olds slugging beer and pouring it gleefully over each other's heads.

Between these two memorable scenes, there's a whole lotta booze: a kid mixes a perfect martini for Coach Buttermaker; the coach collapses and passes out on a baseball diamond littered with empty beer cans.

Buttermaker, like all the adults in *The Bad News Bears*, is corrupt, his soul tainted by life's disappointments. He'd once been a minor league baseball player; now he cleans pools, drinks all day, and ruins relationships. But there is a living scrap of goodness in him. The kids he coaches don't appear innocent, with their potty mouths, violent tendencies, and "grow your own" shirts, but they *are* innocent, and they awaken the latent goodness in him. Buttermaker begins to distinguish himself from the corrupt adults around him: the right-wing club manager who doesn't believe in the equal-opportunity Little League team; the hard-ass rival coach who drives his players to win at any cost, and even smacks his own son on the diamond for a bad play; the wealthy businessman dad who cares only about his career and doesn't have time to coach his son's team, and so instead secretly pays Buttermaker to do a thing that dads are supposed to do, supposed to *want* to do.

While these other adults turn out to be basically irredeemable, Coach Buttermaker has something they don't have: beer. Just kidding. Let's call this thing he has "looseness." It's a quality that is meticulously examined in sociologist Sam Binkley's book *Getting Loose: Lifestyle Consumption in the 1970s*.

The ethos of looseness was disseminated through lifestyle magazines and books like the *Whole Earth Catalog*, a back-to-the-earth guide, or *Mothering*, a journal on midwifery and natural childbirth, or *The Tassajara Bread Book*, a collection of recipes and philosophy by a Zen monk. During the 1970s, the "constraints of tradition" gave way to a new "expressive freedom of the individual," writes Binkley. Loosening was about becoming more authentic and innocent, and it promised a life that was "more primary and immediate but also more active and creative."[3]

Binkley postulates that loosening was a strategy for coping with the anxiety of a changing culture and shifting identities, creating "a small but intact moral universe in which the under-cutting of the traditional foundations of identity and selfhood could be tolerated, even enjoyed, given specific meaning, transformed into a narrative of self-growth and realization told against the backdrop of traumatic twists and turns in the social fabric."[4]

I grew up around adults who were loose like Coach But-termaker. Once my friend Kyla came over to play after school, riding the bus with me to my rural Unionville, Indiana, home. My mom worked from home as a freelance editor, so she was there when we stepped off the bus and she was around as we listened to 45s and ate yogurt-covered pretzels and roamed the land that surrounded our little house. But then my mom drove off to run a quick errand, leaving us on our own. When Kyla's mom arrived to pick her up, she was dismayed to find us kids alone. The next day at school Kyla said she wasn't allowed to come to my house anymore because my mom was a hippie. *What's a hippie?* I asked. *My mom says a hippie is someone who leaves their kids alone*, replied Kyla. It was 1976. The social fabric was twisting and turning, but looseness had not yet caught on in southern Indiana.

Between the Hip and the Square

SLANG WORDS FOR drunk: slammed, wasted, plastered, sloshed, trashed, bombed, hammered.

Also: loose.

In *The Bad News Bears*, Coach Buttermaker's drunkenness can seem both pathetic and heroic. He collapses on the baseball diamond to the disgust of the children. Too loose. But in the end the adult coach and children baseball players merge into one ecstatic beer-drinking heap; in this scene alcohol is equated with heart, joy, humanity, and the cool, hip counterculture—in strong opposition to the tight-assed rival team with their sadistic, square coach.

"Between the hip and the square," writes Binkley, "lay a process of personal change, of loosening up, of becoming loose."[5] The end of *The Bad News Bears* enacts this very tension and transformation.

The one with the booze was who we wanted to be. Who I wanted to be.

The Bad News Bears came out when I was nine (the same

year that Kyla was banned from playing at my house) and I saw it in the theater as a double feature with *Bugsy Malone*, a gangster movie spoof with an all-child cast starring Jodie Foster and Scott Baio. Guns shoot whipped cream, and characters consume bright-colored beverages that are not cocktails but refer to cocktails. This child-heavy double header supported my suspicion that the best life was the life of freedom and independence. The kids in these films had a kind of savvy maturity—they wouldn't have thought anything of a mom leaving her kids alone, or of a kid who wore her house key on yarn around her neck. Eleven-year-old Amanda Whurlitzer, played by Tatum O'Neal, exemplifies this wise-child ideal in *The Bad News Bears*. She swears openly, talks nonchalantly about dating, birth control pills, and going to a Rolling Stones concert. With this wisdom and freedom came a streak of wildness and intoxication, painted not as criminal or dangerous but as liberatory and authentic.

I longed for liberation and authenticity. My mother was loose and trustful enough to leave me home alone with my little brother. But that was the limit of my freedom. Otherwise, I was trapped. I was the weird kid at my conservative, rural elementary school—a freak in a sea of normies. One day I asked the school librarian, *where are the books on astral travel?* A friend of my mom's had told me people can train themselves to fly out of their bodies and travel the universe. Sign me up! The librarian was petite, with a birdlike face and bright pink lipstick. She bent over me, frowning.

Astral travel?

She articulated each syllable, as if I were having trouble understanding her. I wasn't.

We have books on the astroNAUTS?

I fared worse with the kids. My lunches were wrong: too wholesome and grainy; wheat bread with thick, natural peanut butter and honey from the health food co-op, an ugly apple. My clothes were terrible: secondhand corduroys, out of style. I wrote poems, made up stories about being able to communicate with rocks, and talked a lot about playing with my home chemistry set. I had none of the typical girl toys, no Barbie playhouse. Difference was punishable: the punishment was exclusion. And home was no refuge, either. My mom's controlling boyfriend flew into a violent rage if a toy was out of place, a bed unmade, a plateful of broccoli untouched. I was nine and I hated my life, dreamed of running away from home, maybe even leaving my body, floating free into the wide expanse of the universe, but settled for escaping into the universe of *The Bad News Bears* and *Bugsy Malone*.

Some of Us Drink Because We're Not Poets

AMERICANS DRANK HEAVILY through the 1970s, but it was in 1981 that alcohol consumption hit a peak.[6] We were shit-faced in 1981, the year that *Arthur* came out, a movie about a super-rich man who is always shit-faced.

At one moment in the film, a rare moment of darkness, Arthur (played by Dudley Moore) breaks down while talking to the woman he is being forced by his family to marry. *Not all drunks are poets*, he says bitterly to his insipid, adoring fiancée. *Some of us drink because we're not poets.* The scene is jarring because for most of the movie Arthur's drinking is depicted as a charming, boyish affectation, and time after time he emerges cheerful and unscathed from days and nights of blackout-inducing consumption. He drives wasted, swerving off the road, crashing onto the front lawn of his forbidden love interest, the kooky waitress/aspiring actress Linda (Liza Minnelli), before charging screaming into her apartment in the middle of the night. The movie tells us that these gestures are ador-able and romantic, not reckless and rapey. Arthur's drunk-enness is a sign of his sensitivity and superiority. He stands above nearly everyone else in the movie: the uptight business stiffs in his rich father's office, his snooty, lifeless fiancée, his violent, demanding future father-in-law, the sad masses of proletariat (like the unfortunate store security guard who, simply doing his job, confronts Linda when she shoplifts a tie, only to be humiliated by Arthur). Arthur is *better*: innocent, special, loose, almost magical, so pure of heart he laughs like a child in his sleep.

It's not only that he's drunk, of course; he's also rich. Extremely rich, rich enough to escape the consequences of his irresponsible behavior. Watching Arthur forty years later, I find it impossible not to think of Donald Trump, who in 1981 was a thirty-five-year-old New York playboy who never seemed to suffer retribution for his shallow, selfish actions.

Overall, the movie hasn't aged well, but I loved it in 1981. One night my mother dropped me off at the Village Theatre in Bloomington, Indiana, to watch *Arthur* while she went to a nearby laundromat. I was thirteen. I vividly recall the pleasure of watching the movie alone, the luxury of escaping domes-tic drudgery, the enjoyment of a social experience minus any social pressure or obligation, free to step fully out of my life and into the film. This experience established my lifelong love of solo moviegoing—it remains one of my favorite things. When the movie theater in my neighborhood shut down permanently during the pandemic, I cried.

Arthur whispered to my thirteen-year-old heart because I dreamed of living in New York, of being an actress, of being swept off my feet by a quirky, charismatic prince. Dudley Moore's Arthur was adorable, funny, sweet, and he played piano, like the boy I had a crush on at school. It wasn't just his wealth that I found fascinating, but that didn't hurt; I'd grown up with very little money. More than anything, it was his relationship to alcohol that impressed me. Within a year, at fourteen, alcohol would be an important part of my life. When I watched *Arthur*, I was looking ahead, looking for a map to adulthood and wondering what kind of person I wanted to be. Did being drunk equal being romantic, charming, and special? Maybe what I wanted to be was a loveable drunk.

It's Not Fattening and It's Not Good for Me

AMERICA HIT PEAK drunkenness in 1981, but the backlash was coming in the form of Ronald Reagan and Mothers Against Drunk Driving. Soon there would be tougher laws about driving under the influence and public intoxication, as well as a higher minimum drinking age. Some referred to it as an era of "neo-temperance." The following year, 1982, I was fourteen. Things had changed; I'd started having periods and wearing bras. But one thing stayed the same—the glamour of drinking. That year I saw the movie *Tootsie*, and Jessica Lange's character, Julie, swills wine while looking terribly sexy and interesting. When asked why she drinks so much, she answers, *it's not fattening and it's not good for me*. Womanhood could be like that—not constrained or boring, but reckless, unconventional. I loved *Tootsie* for some of the same reasons I loved *Arthur*: the NYC setting, the theater milieu, and the adorable and quirky leading man, in this case Dustin Hoffman. *Tootsie* is steeped in New

York theater culture: acting classes, auditions, soap opera sets, stage productions; it's a movie about actors, and I wanted to be one of them—wild, eccentric, part of a larger creative whole, where difference wasn't punished: difference was celebrated.

My favorite actress at the time was Greta Garbo. I devoured her movies in the wee hours, checking TV listings and staying up all night to watch her, camped out on the couch with a bag of potato chips. She radiated glamour. Garbo had been a sensation as a silent film actress and the camera loved her soulful, expressive face. *Anna Christie*, from 1930, was her first "talkie," marketed with the slogan "Garbo Speaks!" And what did Garbo say? Sitting in a bar, looking impossibly gorgeous and deeply melancholy, her famous first line of dialogue is *Gimme a whiskey*, spoken in a throaty, world-weary voice, with a trace of her Swedish accent intact. *Ginger ale on the side, and don't be stingy, baby!* I stored that line away. I'd try it out myself, years later in a Boston tavern, where it failed to impress the old bartender, who sighed wearily and handed me my drink.

The year I saw *Tootsie* is the year I began to drink, sneakily dipping into my mother's supply at home, watering down the bottles to conceal the transgression, or roaming Bloomington with my friends, looking for someone over twenty-one who might buy us a bottle of Everclear or peach schnapps. Parties were the best. I showed up at my first high school party with my buddy Deeadra. We hadn't been invited, but the word had spread to such an extent that it reached even us, uncool freshmen. We tried to make ourselves look older: me in an extra layer of purple eyeshadow and a cheap, low-cut blouse I bought at the mall (it looked like something a college girl would wear, I thought) and Deedra in thick lip gloss and a stylish cropped sweater she borrowed from her older sister. We were terrified of being turned away, but nobody seemed to care whether we'd been invited or how old we were. We sauntered in and walked freely around the apartment. This was a party. People stood in clumps, talking over loud music (Asia, Toto, Air Supply), holding big red plastic cups of beer. A huge keg sat in the bathtub. Cute boys were everywhere; the more beer I drank, the easier it was to talk to them. I forgot about being young and uncool and overeager and felt myself melt into the scene. I would never be beautiful like Jessica Lange or Greta Garbo. But maybe I could be as drunk, carefree, and alluring?

It was a complicated relationship. One night I'd feel wrapped in a golden glow, smiling and happy, loose and uninhibited enough to be friendly and approachable and bold—sometimes I would even stride up to someone at a party who looked worth knowing. I made lifelong friends this way; I learned how to be social, relieved of my shyness and discomfort. Another night, I'd end up sick and sad, thoroughly disgusted with myself for my loss of control. On a few occasions, I blacked out. This was frightening but also oddly fascinating, to walk and talk and interact, to go places, do things, and have no recollection of any of it. There was a certain freedom to this. I was like Reva Shayne on my favorite soap opera, *Guiding Light*. Reva had launched a new life after she drove off a bridge, her memories and sense of self obliterated by amnesia. Or Sybil, the titular protagonist of a made-for-television movie about a young woman who suffers from multiple personality disorder (now known as dissociative identity disorder), slipping in and out of different identities without any awareness of her other selves. In my twisted adolescent brain, even the darker effects of alcohol held a certain appeal. Not only was alcohol not good for you, but it could change you. It could actually erase you.

I Don't Hate Them . . . I Just Feel Better When They're Not Around

I HAD JUST turned twenty when *Barfly* was released. I loved fringe poet and novelist Charles Bukowski, who wrote the semi-autobiographical script. He was a literary hero to my punk circle of friends, and we passed around *Post Office* (1971) and *Ham on Rye* (1982): smart, pulpy books—cynical, hilarious, and boozy as fuck. *Barfly* follows suit, dramatizing a few days in the life of Bukowski's alter ego, Henry Chinaski (Mickey Rourke, sigh), as he stumbles magnificently from one dodgy bar to another in East Los Angeles. He challenges cheesy bartender Eddie to fist fights in the grimy alley behind his favorite dive while a vivid crowd of drunks cheer them on; meets his damaged but sexy soulmate, Wanda (Faye Dunaway, sigh); allows himself to be courted by a beautiful, rich, young publisher who offers him money, comfort, sex, and an opportunity to publish his stories—some of which he accepts—before returning to his home base in the neon haze, to his fellow barfly friends and to Wanda, who beats the shit out of the pretty publisher and claims Henry as her rightful partner.

When Henry meets Wanda, he asks her what she does. *I drink*, she replies. In 1987 I was living in Boston, playing drums in a band called Blake Babies, and working as a part-time nanny. My circle of fellow travelers were heavy partiers. Drinking was what we did. I was still too young to legally get into a bar, but I had a terrible fake ID that would work in some lowlife joints. Mostly we bought cheap whiskey and gathered in someone's apartment, listening to music, getting sloppy, making eyes at the wrong person, making out with the wrong person, causing trouble. If, the morning after, you don't remember what you did—does it count?

In *Barfly*, drunkenness is noble. Not exactly glamorous, but somehow commendable, a mark of distinction, a signifier of authenticity. *Anybody can be a non-drunk*, says Henry to the sweet young publisher, who doesn't understand why he's squandering his literary talents and destroying his health. *It takes endurance to be a drunk.* His bruised face and slurred speech are badges of honor. There is no virtue in the ability to walk a straight line. Any jerk can do that. In *Barfly*, the body barely matters. Bodies are drowned in alcohol, beaten bloody, starved of nourishment, deprived of sleep. Yet the soul shimmers brightly in spite of—perhaps because of—this neglect. *Some people never go crazy*, writes Henry in a late-night drunken scrawl. *What truly horrible lives they must live.* Unlike Wanda and the other barflies, Henry also writes, beautifully and compellingly. If Arthur drinks because he's not a poet, Henry is a poet because he drinks. And twenty-year-old me idolized writers; I knew a lot of musicians and I was one myself, which made me less inclined to idolize musicians and rock stars who were not, in my estimation, on par with writers. Whatever I wasn't at the moment was what I wanted to be. So it was more than the excessive drinking in *Barfly* that enchanted me, it was also the creative work of the hero, the way he wrote poetic, profound things, blind drunk after a night in the bar. I didn't want to be the beautiful girlfriend Wanda, who just imbibed and didn't do any substantive work. Or the young publisher, who looked for meaning in life by attaching herself to a talented man. I wanted to be Henry. But at the time I had no idea how to be a writer, drunk or sober.

I settled for being simply the drunk, aspiring to the crazy, shimmering glory of the characters in *Barfly*. My attempt landed me in the hospital and then in rehab, which snapped me out of my illusions. Booze wasn't making me shimmer. It was making me sick.

Paṭikūlamanasikāra

I DON'T BLAME all these movies I loved as a kid for the drunk I would become as an adult. But childhood dreams die hard. There's a phenomenon called the reminiscence bump, which means that the music and movies we were devoted to in our teens and twenties imprint more deeply on us than those in any other stage of life, because that is when our brains are most open to absorbing meaning from the world; the project of self-making is in complete overdrive.[7] You'll never forget the words to the songs you loved when you were fourteen or twenty. And I'll never fully recover from the psychic effects of *The Bad News Bears*, *Arthur*, and *Tootsie*, or the delightfully seedy spell of *Barfly*.

Furthermore, research shows that exposure to movies where the heroes drink booze can motivate some viewers, especially adolescents, to consume. Media literacy education is based on the principle that all media messages are embedded with values, stereotypes, and myths, and usually seek to gain profit or power of some type. When we see a character in a film doing something risky, it tends to inspire us to do the same, especially if we identify with and care about that character, or if we think they are entertaining and cool. The solution, according to advocates for media education, is Message Interpretation Processing (MIP). MIP provides a framework for understanding how we are influenced by media messages. A heightened awareness of the ways we internalize these messages can be empowering, inspiring us to analyze and reflect on the effects, thereby reducing the sway of the media's role as a "super peer."[8]

One common step in media literacy programs is to ask students to identify hidden messages in media and then articulate missing information about potential consequences. An advertisement for beer featuring attractive, smiling women implies that drinking beer makes you pretty and happy, but the missing information is that beer can make you overweight (sorry Julie Nichols, it *is* fattening) or sick, or dangerous to yourself and others.

This practice of decoding media reminds me of the unpopular Buddhist practice of Paṭikūlamanasikāra, "reflection on repulsiveness." Paṭikūlamanasikāra explores missing or invisible information, the parts of ourselves and others we don't want to think about. This practice guides the meditator through thirty-two decidedly unglamorous and even disgusting components of the body, including sebum, feces, bile, sweat, and pus. It's a practice recommended as an antidote to lust, one that is said to help the meditator realize that the body is impermanent, always in flux, and always in a state of rotting and decomposition. That hot guy is literally a sack of shit and pus; maybe that will calm your obsession. By some accounts, after the Buddha taught this technique to his followers, some of them killed themselves.[9]

The Buddha's intention wasn't to inspire pain and suicide. The intention was that practitioners of Paṭikūlamanasikāra discover a sense of freedom from bodily attachments and experience greater connection to the shared human experience. It's uncomfortable to see the hot guy as a walking sack of guts; it's also freeing. His power over you diminishes. Now you have some choices to make.

Seeing the beautiful beer-drinking women as sad, sick drunk drivers isn't exactly analogous, I know, but there's a likeness in the practice of looking beyond the surface, observing the things we aren't supposed to observe, discovering more than what we are instructed to see. My quitting booze led me back to childhood, back to the influential super peers of my past, to the forces that helped shape my identity. I was ready to disentangle myself from them and find a new model for my best self and life. One of my own making.

One of These Unlucky People

MY FATHER RECENTLY moved out of his home of thirty years into a condo. In the process of packing, he found a letter I wrote to him from rehab. I wrote that I'd been struggling for three years with alcohol, that I'd tried and failed to quit repeatedly.

> Sunday morning I was extremely sick. I was vomiting for hours. I was deeply depressed, almost suicidal, my head felt as if it were going to explode. I had a hangover from drinking a fifth of whiskey. This is not an uncommon experience for me.

I go on to describe my evening at the walk-in clinic at Beth Israel Hospital in Boston, where a doctor noticed my shaking hands and asked about my drinking habits. *Do you think you are a problem drinker?* she asked me. *Do you have control over alcohol?*

It has control over me, I answered. *But I'm too young to be an alcoholic.*

She asked me if I wanted help, and I said yes, please.

I spent that night in the hospital. They gave me valium for the shakes and hooked me up to an IV full of vitamins. The following morning, I entered a comprehensive alcohol program at St. Elizabeth's Hospital. I wrote the letter on my third day in rehab, still suffering from post-acute withdrawal symptoms.

I'm one of these unlucky people who can't drink, I wrote. *Alcoholism can't be cured.*

I identified as a sober alcoholic for two years after rehab, attending AA meetings, collecting sobriety chips. I'd finally established a healthy relationship with alcohol. The best explanation of why AA works was written in 1972 by the anthropologist Gregory Bateson, who worked in the field of cybernetics, the study of systems. Bateson describes two types of systemic relationships: symmetrical and complementary. In a symmetrical relationship, A and B are equal and similar. If A does something, B then does the same thing, ad infinitum. Bateson gives the example of an arms race as a symmetrical relationship. In a complementary relationship, A and B are dissimilar but fit mutually, like in the cases of dominance-submission or nurturance-dependency. Bateson writes that "there is a strong tendency toward symmetry in the normal drinking habits of Occidental culture. Quite apart from addictive alcoholism, two men drinking together are impelled by convention to match each other drink for drink."[10] But if drinking becomes an addiction, it's impossible to maintain true symmetry. The alcoholic can't drink "normally," can't stop herself when her non-alcoholic friend is ready to stop. Eventually, the primary relationship is between the alcoholic and the bottle, as the alcoholic struggles in vain to stay in control. The reason that AA works for so many, argues Bateson, is that it asks the alcoholic to completely relinquish this illusion of symmetry, to admit powerlessness (the first step of AA), and to surrender to a higher power, as well as to the tenets of AA, accepting a complete shift to a complementary relationship with John Barleycorn.

There's an assumption baked into AA's philosophy that this complementary relationship can never change—an alcoholic will always be an alcoholic. I believe this is true for some. I have friends who are clearly better off living in this state of surrender, and I support them completely. But I don't think it's true for all. In my twenties, I studied macrobiotic diet and philosophy at the Kushi Institute in Massachusetts, and these words from my teacher Michio Kushi have stuck with me:

> Our limited senses delude us into believing that things have a fixed or unchanging quality, in spite of the fact that all of the cells, tissues, skin, and organs that comprise the human body are continuously changing. The red blood cells in the bloodstream live about 120 days. In order to maintain a relatively constant number of these cells, an astounding 200 million new cells are created every

minute, while an equal number of old cells are continuously destroyed. The entire body regenerates itself about every seven years. As a result, what we think of as today's "self" is very different from yesterday's "self" and tomorrow's "self." This is obvious to parents who have watched their children grow. However, our development does not stop when we reach physical maturity: our consciousness and judgment also change and develop during the entire period of life.[11]

Sobriety and AA felt right to me for those two years. And then . . . I quit being sober. My sobriety didn't end with a bender. There was zero drama. I was out with a few new friends one night, they ordered a pitcher of beer, and I drank a glassful. No crazed drunkenness, no spiraling out of control. I'd learned in rehab that ten percent of people can't control themselves with alcohol, can't be "social drinkers." I'd decided back then—quite understandably—that I was one of them. In the year leading up to my hospitalization, my bandmates and friends had begged me to get my drinking under control. I'd wrecked gigs, blown off band practice, lost jobs, damaged and destroyed relationships. I'd developed a tolerance, working my way up to a fifth of whiskey. It made sense to me that I simply had to put the brakes on, raise my hands in surrender. I didn't seem to have a choice. I had to stop.

And yet there I was, a couple of years later with a glass of beer and it was fine. For the remainder of my young adult life I drank without being the kind of problem drinker I'd been pre-rehab. One notable change was that I developed a taste and appreciation for certain kinds of booze, a change that mapped onto my increasing interest in food and cooking. There was more to drinking than getting wasted. I discovered a love for peaty, smoky Scotch and bitter, hoppy ale. I grew attached to the accompanying rituals and accoutrement, finding pleasure in pouring a dram into a tulip-shaped glass with a tapered neck. The aesthetic pleasure and intense taste slowed me down; I didn't pick up the bottle of Scotch and chug. The complementary relationship was altered, and I hovered near the top.

I see in the letter to my dad that my twenty-year-old self was convinced I was a person with the diagnosis of "alcoholic" and that the only way for me to lead a happy, healthy life was to completely abstain and go to meetings. I still feel that I *was* an alcoholic: I had hit bottom when I dragged myself into Beth Israel Hospital, puking and dehydrated and desperate and overflowing with self-loathing. I needed help. I'm grateful I got it. Those two years of sobriety represented a turning point for me as I admitted my powerlessness and switched tracks. I identified as an alcoholic; now I don't. But I've never stopped dancing with this drug. Even through my forties and into my fifties I have, at times, lost that upper hand and suffered damage to my health and happiness. Long nights of insomnia, wretched hangovers, social missteps—like repeating an anecdote multiple times, or bursting into laughter when an acquaintance at a dinner party told me she was undergoing a brutal IRS audit. The worst was when I drank myself into dissociation, which seemed to happen most often at concerts, when I tended to be at my loosest. One summer I saw Brian Wilson, the greatest living singer and songwriter, at the Pitchfork Music Festival. I'd failed to moderate my beer consumption that day, and by the time Wilson's set began I was barely present. I appeared normal to the people around me, but I wasn't really there. I recall only a few moments from the show. And there's no glamour to that erasure. My heavy drinking during Covid lockdown didn't entail a nightly fifth of whiskey, but how would I have answered that kind doctor at Beth Israel had she asked me in January 2021: *do you have control over alcohol?*

Gregory Bateson writes about the AA idea of alcoholic pride, the posturing by the alcoholic that they have self-control even though they know they do not. "The principle of pride-in-risk is ultimately almost suicidal. It is all very well to test once whether the universe is on your side, but to do so again and again, with increasing stringency of proof, is to set out on a project which can only prove that the universe hates you."[12]

I am fiercely determined to lead a sober, healthy life, I wrote to my dad, thirty-four years ago. I haven't led a sober life, as it turns out, but it has been, so far, a largely healthy life. Have I discovered that things aren't as set in stone as my twenty-year-old self thought? Or have I let my twenty-year-old self down?

Jonesing

I DIDN'T HAVE acute withdrawal symptoms when I quit booze in January 2021. It wasn't like when I quit in my twenties. My recent habit of two or three whiskeys a night was easier to kick than that fifth. Even so, I suffered physical symptoms, flu-y sweats and chills and a nasty metallic taste in my mouth, like a bowl of old pennies. I was jumpy and jittery; I'd been slowing my nervous system nightly with alcohol, an effective depressant, and my brain had busily made up for it, overproducing its more stimulating chemicals. I stopped drinking, but the speedy chemicals continued to pump, making me tweaky: I compulsively twirled the ends of my hair, tapped my toes, snapped at Jake when he made himself a cup of tea without offering to make me one. Beware: mad, detoxing drunk slams on the kettle.

The week of flu-y speed gave way to the week of whatever. A dull blank. Nothing particularly irritated me. Nothing pleased me, either. The first sign of real improvement took eight weeks to arrive. I awoke one morning, deeply rested. No sweat-soaked T-shirts by the bed.

God, is this how normal healthy people feel? I asked Jake.

I know, he said. He'd quit drinking years ago, simply because he felt better without it. He'd waited patiently for me to catch up with him in his wisdom.

This is like the best drug ever, I said.

He closed his eyes, held them shut an extra beat, and smiled a satisfied smile. He didn't say, *no shit*. He didn't have to.

I continued to sleep better, which in turn seemed to make me look a little better—eyes and skin clearer, brighter, less red. Let's call that the honeymoon. I absolutely loved not drinking during this phase. I felt free, self-righteous, with the strident glow of the recently reformed. The world beyond my body and apartment looked brighter, too. People were getting vaccinated. The future existed again. Headlines under the new president were almost sweet compared to headlines under the former president. "Biden Announces Free Uber, Lyft Rides to Vaccine Sites." I coasted on the honeymoon for a good while. I wasn't playing gigs or going to parties or going out to dinner. There was less temptation; it was easy to be home and sober. Hangover-free mornings were glorious.

And then a series of events, some good and some terrible, rocked my equilibrium. My dear friend Faith died. The loss would have crushed me regardless, but without my usual coping mechanism it buried me. Later, my mother-in-law died after a long, tough battle with Parkinson's. On the other hand, I finished my MFA, and my band celebrated the release of an album that we'd had to wait over a year to commemorate. I was pleased with myself for being temporarily sober, but it was disorienting to experience these emotional fluctuations without the option of turning to drink for consolation or celebration. Alcohol is so inextricably tied to these heightened moments. It was a moment of extremity—my intense experience watching the inauguration, which was a culmination of fear and stress compounded by years of Trump and Covid—that had pushed me to quit. And it was moments of extremity that most challenged that decision.

Journal Entry: August 10, 2021

I HAVEN'T HAD a drop of alcohol since January. Seven months. Last night I dreamed I broke down and drank a beer at a party, consciously blowing my whole experiment. It was a huge relief to have a drink, a release of pressure, like opening a valve. A comfortable numbing. But there was darkness in the dream, a sense of the way alcohol can diminish your potential—it makes you dumb, sick, slow, and it lets you off the hook of being your best self.

In the dream I felt awful that I'd failed to make it to September 1, the end date for my no-booze experiment. Even still, I sneakily refilled my beer glass, sinking into that familiar feeling that there is never enough, could never be enough.

You know that feeling of relief when you wake up from a distressing dream? I felt that profoundly. I hadn't fucked this particular thing up. I have fucked up so many things before. But I made it this far and I can survive a couple more weeks. It hasn't been easy. Small everyday setbacks like a crappy day at work or negative comments from my thesis reader ignite the desire to drink. And the big, difficult losses are backbreaking. Faith's death. Weezie's death. It has been bewildering to navigate sorrow without drinking, such a bare, raw feeling, nowhere to turn. Nothing to take the edge off, just feeling my way through.

I spend so much time now anticipating that first drink on September 1 that I wonder if these obsessive thoughts are almost as anesthetizing as actually drinking. All this yearning, all this looking forward. I can't wait to feel less.

I had my babies unmedicated—I wanted to feel them being born. I've spent much of my life high, numb, unfeeling. I wanted to be present for that experience, even if it hurt. Is there some way to apply this logic to the rest of my life? Been numb long enough. Time to feel my way through.

I miss drinking. When a gang of family members went to a pub after my mother-in-law's funeral, I was jealous, and later that night the bottle of whiskey on the kitchen counter looked delicious and golden. At the same time, I relished my calm and sobriety. With drinking, it's usually better if it's all for one, one for all. I think of my former bandmate Juliana, who never drank as we partied heavily around her. How monstrous we must have looked, especially me, who always went too far, could never stop. Being the sober person in a roomful of drunk people is strange. The behavior of those around me disintegrates, becomes grotesque, their faces redden, their voices rise in pitch.

That used to be me. That was always, always me.

We're All Drinking Poison

TWO BOOKS KEPT me company during my sober months: *Quit Like a Woman* by Holly Whitaker and *Drunk* by Edward Slingerland. They quarreled with each other. I played both sides.

Whitaker, who has been sober since 2013, has said that alcohol is "just a cheap substitute for real life."[13] *Quit Like a Woman* questions our cultural assumptions that all drinkers can be divided into two categories: healthy people who can drink with no problem, and alcoholics. Whitaker argues that we are all unlucky when it comes to booze, that *nobody* can drink without consequence—alcohol is ethanol, she reminds us, and drinking it is like drinking engine fuel: "It's actually poison. We're all drinking poison."[14]

She meticulously details the damaging effects of ethanol consumption, offering a list that she writes should "come at the end of every Corona commercial and winery tour." Alcohol disrupts sleep, fuels anxiety, impedes detoxification, causes weight gain, causes facial redness, damages your brain, messes with blood sugar balance, disrupts endocrine function, is linked to seven different cancers, causes premature aging, and destroys your microbiome.[15]

Whitaker sums it up: "What I'm saying is: Booze fucks our shit up."

The distinction between a "healthy" or "alcoholic" drinker is irrelevant to Whitaker. "The words alcohol and alcoholism need to burn," she writes. "To be clear, I believe that alcohol is addictive, that alcohol addiction is progressive, that some people are wired a bit differently and are more vulnerable to alcohol addiction. . . . I'm not refuting that alcohol addiction is an actual thing. . . . What I'm saying is that alcohol is addictive to everyone."[16] She critiques many of the accepted theories of addiction while offering alternative perspectives, including those of addiction recovery expert Tommy Rosen, who argues that addiction is the state of being disconnected from our minds and bodies; it is the opposite of awareness, and it is any behavior you continue to do despite the fact that it brings negative consequences.

I love the way Whitaker digs deep to ask why she drank, why any of us drink. "I spent a year chasing down the question why am I an alcoholic? Before I started chasing down the questions that matter, like why can't I be with myself at all?"[17] She doesn't offer pat answers: "The reason you are turning to a substance to cope is as complicated as you are, and the only way you can get at what is causing you to need to numb out and escape is to look at the things that are driving that discomfort and to start adding solutions there."[18]

She describes the solutions that worked for her—finding meaningful work, practicing intense yoga, cultivating deeper friendships, establishing nourishing daily rituals. The crux of the book, for me, is Whitaker's argument that, in order to heal from addiction, "We need to create a life we don't need to escape."[19] This sentiment haunted me. I thought of little Freda and her quest for astral travel. What would a life I didn't need to escape look like?

I appreciate Whitaker's brisk fanaticism and confidence. She waits for the world to catch up to her, convinced that booze is in for its own "cigarette moment"—a public rejection and reversal of popular opinion, relegating alcohol to the past as something we used to do before we fully realized how harmful it was.

In the meantime, most of us have a long way to go. Whitaker describes the challenge of telling friends she doesn't drink, observing that this tends to raise defenses, a threat. I noticed this myself. Some people squirmed when I told them about my break from alcohol and launched into either an apology for or defense of their own drinking habits. One friend took the news defiantly, describing her daily walk to the liquor store, where she bought a bottle of wine and a few minis of hard stuff.

I only buy what I can drink in one day, she said.

That didn't sound healthy; should I say something? I hadn't the right to judge. A daily walk to the liquor store had been built into my life, once. I suddenly felt self-conscious that

I wasn't drinking, worried that I was acting the way I felt, which was slightly superior. I overcompensated by downplaying my quitting.

It's only temporary, I said. *I'll be back on the bottle again in a few months.*

There's no way to deflect this kind of self-scrutiny. I think Whitaker would say it's because many of us know deep down that we have a complicated relationship with John Barleycorn.

And Wine unto Them That Be of Heavy Hearts

EDWARD SLINGERLAND ARGUES that our very evolution as humans is intimately linked to our relationship with booze. He quotes archaeologist Patrick McGovern's joke/not joke that our species ought to be referred to as "*Homo imbibens*."[20] Maybe you were taught that the earliest farmers domesticated grain to make bread? The bread might have been an afterthought. Beer seems likely to have come first.

Slingerland concedes that alcohol is damaging, dangerous, and addictive. But why do we love it so much? Why have we always loved it? Why haven't we evolved into teetotalers by now if it's so bad for us? Slingerland believes that there are solid evolutionary reasons for why *Homo imbibens* is still going strong. "It might actually be good for us to tie one on now and then,"[21] he writes. There are three basic reasons why this is so: alcohol makes us more creative; alleviates stress; and builds trust, "pulling off the miracle of getting fiercely tribal primates to cooperate with strangers."[22] Alcohol deactivates the part of our brain that keeps us in line, the prefrontal cortex, our "seat of cognitive control." Intoxication "is an antidote to cognitive control, a way to temporarily hamstring that opponent to creativity, cultural openness, and communal bonding."[23] In language that recalls Sam Binkley's analysis of the 1970s, Slingerland declares, "We need to become looser—one of Dionysus' alternative names in Latin was *Liber*; 'The Free.'"[24]

Going back to Holly Whitaker, she would agree with Leo Tolstoy's essay "Why Do Men Stupefy Themselves?" which postulates that the attraction of intoxicants is "not in the taste, nor in any pleasure, recreation, or mirth they afford, but simply in man's need to hide from himself the demands of conscience."[25] Whitaker describes several relatable incidents in which she deliberately got drunk in order to fuck someone she oughtn't. But Slingerland waves a friendly mug of beer at this kind of thinking. "What is being fled," he argues, "is not one's conscience but rather the harshness of everyday life."[26] The Christian Bible backs him up: "Give strong drink unto him that is ready to perish, and wine unto them that be of heavy hearts. Let him drink, and forget his poverty, and remember his misery no more."[27]

Aldous Huxley joins the chorus in his autobiography, *The Doors of Perception*:

> That humanity at large will ever be able to dispense with Artificial Paradises seems very

unlikely. Most men and women lead lives at the worst so painful, at the best so monotonous, poor and limited that the urge to escape, the longing to transcend themselves if only for a few moments, is and always has been one of the principal appetites of the soul.[28]

Huxley's point about longing to transcend reminds me of the band I worshipped during my heaviest drinking years, the Bukowski of bands, poetic and trashed: the Replacements, of course. I saw them live at every opportunity and marveled at their shambolic mess. At one show, guitarist Bob Stinson careened onstage mid-set dressed in a Peter Pan costume and waving a bottle of Wild Turkey, which he passed through the audience (you bet I took a swig). This band was perfect, the way they celebrated ragged pain, shouted out heartbreak, dug into despair to transcend it. Alcohol was central to the alchemy. In the achingly beautiful "Here Comes a Regular," Paul Westerberg sings about the intense thirst a person can work up after "a hard day of nothing much at all."

It's unlikely that Westerberg was deliberately invoking Friedrich Nietzsche, but "Here Comes a Regular" does seem to rhyme with the philosopher's sentiment that drunkenness releases us from "the horror of individual existence."[29] Nietzsche saw the value in this escape, especially for the enslaved and alienated, but he also considered it a disadvantage and weakness: ideally we are able to face the horror of existence with strength and sobriety.

Slingerland's voice is a tad milder than Westerberg's and Nietzsche's; he argues winningly for a compromise: "Intoxication is in itself the opportunity for a temporary escape from the moderation that the rest of life is necessarily mortgaged to." There is value, he argues, in the occasional "vacation from the self."[30]

I'm all in favor of the vacation from the self. My favorite part of Slingerland's argument, though, is that "intoxication is its own justification."[31] Life has been particularly hard lately, and we might need to have our unconscious opened like a flower on a semi-regular basis. Perhaps intoxication could be classified as a fourth basic human drive, after food, sex, and sleep. In Andrew Weil's 1972 book, *The Natural Mind*, he claims that we are all "born with a drive to experiment with ways of changing consciousness."[32] Even young children seek intoxication, spinning around until they collapse, dizzy and laughing. If intoxication is a natural need, is my project of quitting everything unnatural?

I have always loved being high. One night when I was ten years old, I awoke with an excruciating stomachache. My mother gave me a sliver of a codeine tablet, and within the hour my pain entirely vanished. Magic. I was almost ecstatic, drifting sweetly through the night. I'd felt this shade of happiness before as a child: NyQuil, Robitussin. A syrupy softness that spreads through your being. Relief. The profoundest relief. When I discovered alcohol as a teenager, I also discovered a similar feeling, finding the escape and transcendence that Huxley describes, the vacation from the self that I had sought since childhood. This drive to intoxication is core to my being. At times I have resisted it, denied it, even battled with it. At times I've taken a prudent and productive step back from it. But I return to this: I very much like to get high. I have always been a person who likes to get high.

Maxima vs. Optima

GREGORY BATESON COMPARES Alcoholics Anonymous to General Motors in that the organization has one purpose and is dedicated to maximizing that purpose, which, for AA, is "to carry the AA message to the sick alcoholic who wants it." Bateson is pro-AA, but argues that this kind of maximalization is unnatural. "In biology there are no values that have the characteristic that if something is good, then more of something will be better. Economists seem to think that this is true of money but, if they are right, money is thereby shown to be certainly unbiological and perhaps antibiological. . . . For the rest, good things come in optima, not maxima."[33] He offers the example of a redwood forest: "There is no single variable in the redwood forest of which we can say that the whole system is oriented to maximizing that variable and all other variables are subsidiary to it; and indeed, the redwood forest works toward optima, not maxima. Its needs are satiable, and too much of anything is toxic."[34]

Even too much oxygen will kill you.

Fuck-Marry-Kill

THE GAME FUCK-MARRY-KILL, where you're given three names of potential love or sex interests and required to place each in one of the above categories, has always bothered me. Can't we have a "flirt" option? A "tango" option? One of the advantages of quitting is that it creates space: breaking out of the daily habit of drinking let me step away and view it with fresh eyes and a sense of curiosity. It didn't leave me with absolute clarity. Alcohol is poison and I was cleaner and healthier without. Yes. And. Alcohol is medicine and I was bereft and diminished without. I've been alive long enough to not expect absolute clarity in anything. After decades in a relationship with John Barleycorn, I don't want to fuck, marry, or kill him. I think what I want is to stay conscious and keep dancing.

Sugar

That Stuff Is Poison

FOR CHRISTMAS 1992, I gave out copies of William Dufty's 1975 *Sugar Blues* to friends and family. I considered it life-altering reading. I was, I should add, a self-righteous and preachy prig, but I didn't know it. I'd spent half of that year working and studying at the Kushi Institute, a macrobiotic community in a rustic, rambling old house—a former monastery—in the Berkshire mountains of Western Massachusetts, and out there we all agreed that sugar was bad news, both drug and poison. *Sugar Blues* was a canonical text to us, and copies of it sat on the community shop shelves next to organic whole-foods cookbooks. Back home in Bloomington, I remained fanatically anti-sugar, failing to notice that those around me didn't share my fanaticism. One of those copies of *Sugar Blues* went to my father-in-law, a professor of religious studies at Indiana University. He was considerate enough to read it and honest enough to tell me he didn't think much of Dufty's writing. He was particularly put off by the author conflating the identities of Muhammad, the prophet of Islam, with Elijah Muhammad, the twentieth century leader of the Nation of Islam. I should have been more embarrassed than I was. The other people I gave it to didn't even crack it open.

I recently reread the book. It's utterly bonkers, although it opens with a fantastic scene: Dufty finds himself in a press conference alongside legendary actress Gloria Swanson. He unwraps a sugar cube to stir into his coffee and she hisses at him, *that stuff is poison*.[35] Dufty comes to agree—and later marries Swanson. The book briefly details his woes and ills before the relief he finds by eliminating sugar from his life. Who can resist a good makeover narrative? But Dufty goes further, expanding his argument to examine a host of humanity's woes and ills, all of which he links to the poisonous white stuff. Sugar is implicated not only for dental cavities, obesity, and diabetes, but also highway fatalities, slavery, cancer, alcohol and drug addiction, freckles, sunburn, mosquito bites, witch trials, and all forms of mental illness. It is outlandish, reckless, almost obscene. But let me be clear: I totally love this book.

As paranoid and unsubstantiated as Dufty's claims often are, we would all benefit from a healthy dose of paranoia when it comes to sugar, especially in terms of the powerful entities who have profited from selling it. In the 1940s, scientists at Harvard University were paid off by the sugar industry to publish the results of a study suggesting that fat and cholesterol were the key causes of heart disease and to suppress the results of a study showing that sugar was even more of a factor in heart health and a direct cause of obesity. We are still living with the effects of this intentional misdirection and blatant bribery, which shaped public health policy and gave us the recommendation for a high carbohydrate, low-fat diet—a diet that has resulted in a dramatic increase in obesity and heart disease in the U.S. Recent studies support the findings of the suppressed 1940s study: people who consume a quarter of their daily calories from sugar are more than twice as likely to die from heart disease. It's not outlandish to claim that millions have suffered and died because of the shady doings of Big Sugar.[36]

I Quit Sugar

DURING MY FIRST booze-free month I eased the pain of sobriety with homemade cookies, an extra pour of maple syrup on my pancakes, fruit juice in my spritzer, and bars of good dark chocolate. This is an old trick of sober drunks. I haven't been to an AA meeting since the '80s, so maybe things have changed, but meetings used to be fueled by huge urns of crappy coffee with all the off-brand sugar cubes you wanted, and cellophane-swaddled packages of sugar cookies. The "Big Book" of Alcoholics Anonymous explicitly pushes sweets when the craving for alcohol hits. Sugar is soothing and comforting, but there's more to it. My habit of piling cheap-ass cookies on my napkin at AA meetings was biologically driven. Sugar diminishes cravings for alcohol in some people: sugar—like nicotine, cocaine, heroin, and alcohol—activates the brain's reward center, stimulating the release of dopamine. Rats will consistently choose sugar over cocaine, even when they're addicted to cocaine. Monkeys too.[37]

It makes sense that we'd be hardwired to seek out sugar. For many of us, our first taste of anything is breast milk, which is incredibly sweet, a melted milkshake with extra sugar. Sweetness is rare in nature, and historically we had to work hard to get it. Nowadays it's inexpensive, plentiful, and processed. The sugar we eat, whether it's refined sugar cane, beet sugar, or high fructose corn syrup, comes to us in a concentrated form that intensifies and magnifies the heady effect on our brains.

We might not think of sugar as a drug because it's so ubiquitous. But it is. And I felt like absolute crap when I kicked it.

In February 2021, I went cold turkey, eliminating not only refined sugar but also natural sources like honey and maple syrup. Even fruit got the ax. I wanted a complete reset. This was incredibly challenging; I hadn't thought my normal diet included all that much sugar until I stopped eating it and realized that my granola, dark chocolate, Thai food, and bottled smoothies had to go. I wasn't surprised that avoiding sugar was a pain, but I was shocked by how terrible I felt. For three long weeks I was listless, achy, and faintly nauseated, the way I'd been in the early days of pregnancy, constantly nibbling on crackers to settle my stomach. Quitting sugar required all-day vigilance, which was very different from quitting booze—I didn't think much about alcohol until nightfall. Sugar was in my face from sunrise to sunset, when Jake drizzled honey on his yogurt and I ate mine plain, or when an afternoon slump hit hard and I couldn't turn to a reviving piece of chocolate. I had physical cravings for sugar, much more so than I did for alcohol. Sugar-free living brought out my inner whiny child. After all, we went way back, me and sugar. It was my first drug. And the first cut is the deepest.

O Cap'n! My Cap'n!

I CAN'T THINK of a more apt synecdoche for my Gen X childhood than Saturday Morning Cartoons. This was a parent-free zone, no helicoptering oversight or protection. My brother and I, awake long before the grown-ups, sat with bowls of Cheerios, absorbing hours of entertainment made just for us. My favorite Saturday morning show featured live actors and puppets in a wild psychedelic world populated by animate trees, houses, mushrooms, clocks, and lollipops. This was the backdrop to an ongoing battle between the innocent Jimmy—who was stranded in this strange world and aided by a magical talking flute and a friendly dragon—and the wicked Witchipoo. The name of this fabulous show, *H.R. Pufnstuf*, was an intentional reference to marijuana that had been intended as a prank on "clueless NBC executives,"[38] as were the lyrics of the theme song, which vaguely declares how hard it is to "do a little" of something, "'cause you can't do enough." It all went over my head as much as it did the squares at NBC. I was there for the colorful, mystical mayhem.

I had favorite cartoons too, especially *Scooby-Doo* and

Super Friends. Strangely, though, my most vivid memories are of the commercials, which functioned as a proto-Facebook experience, inspiring complex surges of longing, pain, delight, and exclusion.

It was all about the cereal.

While I ate my Cheerios, the breakfast our health-conscious mother allowed us, I gazed at cartoon ads for multicolored Trix, its naughty rabbit and condescending kids: *Silly rabbit, Trix are for kids!* Well, not all kids; not me. Just the lucky ones. Lucky Charms was a bowl full of sugary marshmallows that were *magically delicious*, a sprightly leprechaun promised. I craved color, beauty, magic. Not beige, bland, soggy O's.

The live action commercials got to me even more: the Honeycomb Hideout was my Shangri-La—cool kids wearing cool clothes in a cool clubhouse. Their snappy song was infectious: *Honeycomb's big (yeah yeah yeah), It's not small (no no no).* I envied the lives these kids seemed to live, especially their bowls of sticky, sweet, crunchy cereal.

These were powerful and effective media messages. Very young viewers have a hard time telling the difference between bright, animated commercials and regular cartoon programming, and these lines are intentionally blurred to inspire kids to pressure their parents into buying the cereals. I for sure put pressure on my mom. I got nowhere.

This left me fiendish. I ate sugary breakfast cereal at every opportunity—sleepovers with friends, visits with my kind, indulgent grandmother. Cap'n Crunch was my darling. I dreamed of a future when I'd start every single day with multiple bowls of Cap'n Crunch. My Cap'n! I would follow you to the ends of the earth. Even though you violently shred the inside of my mouth. I don't care. I'm yours.

Sugar Swings

CEREAL WAS JUST one of the advertised and coveted foods not allowed in our home; we also couldn't have artificially flavored, preservative-laden snacks like Twinkies, or teeth-rotting soda. At one elementary school birthday party I drank nine sodas in a few hours, chugging them down like a wild alcoholic (maybe inspired by Coach Buttermaker). We played kick the can and I charged around elated, indefatigable, high as a kite.

*

"EXHAUSTION MAY BE dangerous," reads the sidebar to an advertisement in *Time* magazine. "Especially in children who haven't learned to avoid it by pacing themselves. Exhaustion opens the door a little wider to the bugs and ailments that are always lying in wait. Sugar puts back energy fast—offsets exhaustion. . . . Energy is the first requirement of life. Play safe with your young ones—make sure they get sugar every day."

This ad is from 1964, three years before I was born. Health researchers at the time agreed that sugar caused obesity and diabetes, and this advertising campaign was Big Sugar's expensive pushback. The sidebar alone is astonishing, but the ad itself is truly surreal. It features an attractive, smiling, white teenage girl in a sweater and tweed skirt, in the middle of a dance step, snapping her fingers, hair flying. "Mary got to school early for student council. Her team won in gym. After play rehearsal, she'll Watusi with the gang. She needs sugar in her life. For energy. . . . Sugar swings. Serve some."[39]

The Circle of Life

I WAS EMBARRASSED when friends came to my house and asked for a Coke. All we had in the fridge was milk and orange juice. Of course, when I became a mother I never once bought soda, Honeycomb cereal, or Twinkies for my kids. I was probably even stricter than my mom about food. But as a kid I felt deprived and weird and left out. All of which fed a longing that grew to be almost erotic.

Sugar Pie, Honey Pie

SEVERAL EXAMPLES OF the ways in which sugar and honey have always been metaphors for love and sex:

1. In the Old Testament poem cycle "Song of Solomon," the husband praises his beloved wife: *Your lips, O my spouse, Drip as the honeycomb: Honey and milk are under your tongue.* (Ronnie Milsap's 1974 hit "Pure Love" offers a twentieth-century update, comparing love to milk, honey, and my old favorite, Cap'n Crunch.) The lines in "Song of Solomon" can be interpreted in a couple of different ways (and some Christians say the whole thing is an allegory for the love between Christ and the Church; boring): either those are some extremely kissable lips, or those lips are speaking sweet words of love. Either way: total fire.

2. The word "honeymoon" refers to a wine made from fermented honey that was recommended to newly

married couples as an aphrodisiac (and "moon" signified a month dedicated to drinking wine and making love).[40]

3. We effortlessly slip into sugary language when talking about romance—we call a lover sweetheart, honey, sugar pie.

4. There are countless songs ostensibly about sugar but actually about sex: "Sugar, Sugar" by the Archies, "No Sugar Tonight" by the Guess Who, "I Want Candy" by Bow Wow Wow, "Watermelon Sugar" by Harry Styles, and many, many, many more.

5. When I lived in England in the aughts, I was often asked to answer for American policy and culture. *What are you going to do about the war in Iraq?* people would ask me. *When are you going to close Guantánamo?* On a lighter note, a friend held me personally responsible for what she saw as the scandalous, sexual names of popular American snack foods. *Twinkies??* she said. *Ding Dongs?? HoHos??* She was outraged. I'd never noticed this before, but I had to admit it looked bad.[41]

As She's Walking Out the Door

SEXUAL OBSESSION TENDS to be most consuming when the object of desire is inaccessible or forbidden. My devotion to Cap'n Crunch faltered the moment I became an adult and could eat whatever I wanted. The charge was gone, yet something lingered, even if it was only a memory of longing—a sweet, crunchy space in the corner of my heart.

Angels and Devils

THE WORD "DEVIL" probably originates from "deva" (masculine) and "devi" (feminine), Vedic divinities that represent various forces of nature or human virtues. In India, the devas and devis rose in prominence and are still held in high esteem; popular devas include Shiva, Ganesha, and Hanuman. But as the concept spread out of India, the fate of the devas evolved. In the Middle East, they were denounced by Zoroaster, the founder of Zoroastrianism, who deemed them malignant forces. In Persia they became divs or devs, monstrous creatures, and in Christian Europe they became the Devil.[42]

Devas and devis are evolving still and have found a place in modern, nature-based religions like Wicca. Wiccan writer Thea Summer Deer describes them as "the architects of life, they are the unseen, other side of nature."[43] In this belief system, plants have spirits and personalities.

Let's say sugar has a spirit, a personality. What is the nature of the sugar deva? We associate sweetness with, among other things, divinity—perhaps inspired by our sweet mother's milk and the historical rarity of sweetness. Even sugarcane itself, in its unrefined form, must have seemed a gift from Heaven, with its sweet juice and enlivening effects. Now, though, every American consumes over one hundred pounds a year,[44] which rots our teeth and makes us fat and sick.

Satan himself was God's favorite before his fall. Is every devil a fallen angel?

Too Yang

DURING MY SUGAR withdrawal, I did not swing, nor did I Watusi. Instead, I nodded off on the floor during Zoom meetings and dragged my sorry, sober, sugar-free ass around as best I could, trusting that something good would come of this.

I loosened up after the first sugar-free month, allowing fresh fruit back into my diet and enjoying an occasional sweet treat baked with brown rice syrup, a mellow, fermented, honey-like sweetener favored by old-school macrobiotics. I didn't want deprivation to reignite my childhood sugar freak, and the little bit of fruit and rice honey helped me feel slightly less sorry for myself as I passed on chocolate mousse at restaurants and turned down homemade peach pie baked by my dad's friend and neighbor, who happens to be the best baker I know. Quitting alcohol had triggered vehement responses from others. The responses to quitting sugar were milder. To borrow Holly Whitaker's language, sugar may be having its "cigarette moment." Some of the trendiest current diets, including Keto,

Paleo, and Whole30, strictly forbid the consumption of refined sugar. My dad's friend asked why I was skipping the peach pie, but he seemed satisfied with my response that I was "detoxing."

We all want sweetness. Food is more than nutrition and fuel. Remember when Sarah Palin brought two hundred cookies to a Pennsylvania elementary school? Your nice, fun mommy brings cookies. Your uptight, mean mommy brings carrot sticks. Palin was striking out at First Lady Michelle Obama's campaign for healthy eating and exercise, a project that included a well-publicized vegetable garden at the White House. (Donald Trump tore that garden out, the way Ronald Reagan tore Jimmy Carter's solar panels off the White House roof.)

When you're hooked on sugar, the sugar deva is part of you; you believe in him, defend him. When you kick sugar, the spirit eventually leaves you. You turn against him.

Back when I was living at the Kushi Institute, I ate the cleanest possible diet: whole grains, vegetables, miso soup, beans and other pulses, and a little fish and fruit. By comparison, the Standard American Diet looked like pathetic baby food: sweet, milky, oily, sticky. And it looked poisonous: chemical-laden, dyed, artificially flavored, processed beyond recognition, and wrapped in plastic. There's something powerful, dignified, and pure about the austerity of a bowl of well-cooked brown rice. Set that bowl of rice next to a glowing orange bowl of Kraft macaroni and cheese.

Honestly, though—that level of purity can make you insufferable. The fundamental principles of life, according to macrobiotics, are yin and yang. Everything can be understood through these opposite, complementary tendencies. Yin produces cold, darkness, expansion, openness. Yang produces heat, light, constriction, tightness. Yin is lunar, yang is solar. In terms of the substances we ingest, the most yin things are sugar, alcohol, and drugs. The most yang are fish, meat, and salt. The most balanced between the two polarities are whole grains and vegetables.

The first two months of quitting found me eliminating two of the most yin substances in my life, alcohol and sugar. Was I becoming too yang? Calling someone "too yang" was the commonest insult at the Kushi Institute. We were all pretty yang there, eating a narrow, healing diet of mostly plants, working hard in the gardens and kitchen all day, avoiding drugs, sugar, and alcohol. Sometimes someone would become so obviously tight, rigid, inflexible, irritated with everything and everyone, that an intervention was required. This usually came in the form of advice: *eat nabe* (nabe is a relaxing dish of lightly boiled vegetables in broth, considered to be yinnizing). Other advice might be *drink a beer* or *go out for dinner and eat whatever you want—no rules!*

But during my experiment, I was living in a world of rules.

Steady and Sweet

STHIRA AND SUKHA are ancient Indian terms that likely predate the terms yin and yang. In the *Yoga Sutras*, written sometime between 200 BCE and 200 CE by the Indian sage Patanjali (often referred to as the father of yoga), we read that yoga practice is "Sthira Sukham." A common English translation of this is "The posture of yoga is steady and easy."[45] Sthira means steadiness, effort, and strength. Sukha means ease, comfort, and sweetness. The balance between these elements is essential to yoga. On the one end of the spectrum, too much effort creates an aggressive practice with the risk of injury and oblivion to the subtleties of yoga practice. At the other end, too much comfort creates an aimless, drifting practice, with no momentum or power.

Steadiness + Sweetness = Magic

The Twinkie Theory

THE TWINKIE THEORY,[46] conceived of by my friend Janas, suggests that since we don't live in a pure, perfect world, we therefore shouldn't eat a pure, perfect diet. Eat mostly heathy food but throw in the occasional Twinkie. It's a little bit homeopathic, this theory: a tiny amount of poison is the cure. It reminds me of our advice at the Kushi Institute to eat nabe or drink beer. Have rules; bend them as necessary.

Beauty and Sweetness

MY FRIENDS DANIEL and Catherine went to a bar mitzvah and told me about how candy was thrown at the bar mitzvah'd youth, family and loved ones showering the young man with sweetness, easing his transition to adulthood. Similarly, there's a tradition of Jewish parents smearing honey on a child's first schoolbook, to imprint upon the child that learning is sweet. And there's a tradition of throwing fruits on the holiday Simchat Torah to celebrate the beauty and sweetness of the Torah.

In his elegant and gloomy song "Hospital," about a lover who has suffered a mental breakdown, Jonathan Richman sings about going to bakeries all day long to fill the void of sweetness in his life. An early Buddhist axiom, quoted in *Sugar Blues*, counters Richman:

> If you look for sweetness
> Your search will be endless
> You will never be satisfied

But if you seek the true taste

You will find what you're looking for[47]

Living sugar-free felt amazing, eventually. I do think it's both poison and drug, and our bodies are better off without it. I lost several pounds of Covid weight just by quitting sugar, and my menopause symptoms, which had eased in the absence of alcohol, continued to improve: fewer hot flashes, less night sweat. Still, I am occasionally captivated by the sugar deva. He reminds me about the value of pure pleasure to be found in a tall, frosted cake or a slice of cold apple pie; and he reminds me about the futility of striving for perfection in an imperfect world. He tells me straight up that people who quit sugar can be hugely judgmental dicks (and he's looking at me). And he says come on, honey. Have a cookie.

Cannabis

Legalized It

BACK IN THE late 1980s, I sprayed mace in a boyfriend's face as a joke. Was I drunk? Righteously angry? How could I do such an awful thing?

I didn't. It never happened. When I brought it up years later, the boyfriend laughed and corrected me. I carried mace, a gift from my brother to keep me safe in the big city when I moved to Boston. But I never once used it. I must have thought about it, or maybe I wanted to do it, or dreamed about it, and that thought or desire or dream grew into a false memory. Is it just as bad to think about something as it is to do it? After all, coveting is a sin.

Anyway, I'm at a point in my life where I remember things that didn't happen.

Still, I trust one particular memory. It was January 1, 2020, and I felt optimistic. This would be the year that Trump would be voted out of office, possibly impeached, maybe even imprisoned. This would be the year that my band Sunshine

Boys would release our second album; we'd planned local gigs, national tours. And this was the year that weed finally became legal for recreational use in Illinois. On New Year's Day, I was overjoyed as I waited in an hours-long dispensary line in the freezing cold, toes and fingers numb, standing with men, women, young, old, Black, brown, and white.

What a great year this was going to be.

(Not) High School

I HAD NOT always been so excited about marijuana. I was not a high school pothead. Pot was unpredictable; sometimes it was benign, giggly fun, sitting atop a McDonald's jungle gym with Deeadra, sharing an order of Chicken McNuggets, marveling over the perfection of the sauces. Sweet and Sour. Barbecue. Oh my god. Usually weed was disappointing—dusty joints that only resulted in a headache. At one high school party, I took a long bong hit and wound up immobilized on a grubby couch in a cold sweat, occasionally whimpering, completely miserable. A kind friend stayed by my side, threw a blanket on me, and protected me, occasionally petting my head like I was a sad, sick kitty cat.

Alcohol and caffeine were my drugs of choice; I knew what to expect from them and usually knew what I could handle.

My boyfriend, on the other hand, was a classic high school pothead. The issue became contentious. I hated when he smoked around me, hated that remote, vapid affect, the way his eyes would half close and he'd laugh at everything, while seeming not to grasp a word I said. There was something terrifying about his being both there and not there. I petulantly demanded that he relinquish the habit. I didn't even want him to smoke when we were apart, which seems ludicrous and controlling to me now. Somehow it seemed reasonable to my stupid teen self: if he loved me, he'd stop.

I was seventeen when *The Breakfast Club* came out. I was charmed and stirred by it, couldn't help but have crushes on the entire cast. But I took issue with the way the narrative was activated by the characters getting high together. I didn't like how smoking a joint was like a magic potion that allowed them to lower their defenses, discover their shared humanity, and connect as true friends. It was a common trope at the time: films like *Revenge of the Nerds*, *9 to 5*, *The Big Chill*, and *Romancing the Stone* all feature pivotal moments in which getting high changed the dynamic of a scene or relationship, and always for the better. What a prude I was when it came to weed! I even disapproved of *Up in Smoke*, Cheech and Chong's 1978 stoner classic, a favorite of a few of my friends. I like the movie now (especially when I'm high), but back then I found its portrayal of potheadism squalid and goofy, and it lacked political power, delivered no real punch to the man. I was much more attracted to punk rock, smart and edgy and in total opposition to stoned hippie culture. It wasn't a very sophisticated line of reasoning, but my budding punk sensibility strengthened my antiweed stance. I lacked discipline and gravitated towards the Dionysia, but I admired the "straight-edge" punks; they took no bullshit, they worked hard, and they displayed a clarity and intensity that I venerated, as exemplified by the Washington, DC band Minor Threat's legendary lead singer, Ian MacKaye, who sang/ yelled with venom and gusto that he didn't drink, smoke, or fuck, but at least he could "fucking think!"

The T-O

TOM WAS MY mom's boyfriend. He lived with my mother and brother and me during most of my elementary school years, and I was afraid of him, for good reason. I'm pretty sure he was a drug dealer; he was determined to produce a crop of homegrown on the acre of land that surrounded our house. He planted cannabis seeds in the middle of the corn plot, intending to spell his name, but he ran out of seeds two-thirds of the way through the letters.

My brother and I had chores: pull weeds, feed the chickens, and water the T-O. The plants exploded in the Indiana summer; later they would hang upside down to dry in the barn out back, sun shining through the wood slats, exposing thick clouds of pollen. I'm guessing we got high just standing in that barn, breathing.

Mom and Tom had parties. The grown-ups were there and not there. They used dollar bills to roll joints and sometimes left the coiled-up money on a coffee table, forgotten. I surreptitiously snatched those bills up, squirrelled them away, used them to buy ice cream when a nice babysitter would drive us into town. We got our fix, too.

Alien Robot

SEVEN YEARS AGO, an old friend—the very boyfriend I'd border-
line bullied in high school for his love of smoking pot—gave me
a piece of gummy candy in the shape of an alien robot with
delineated arms, legs, head, and torso. *If you eat this whole thing,
you'll wind up in the E.R.*, he said. *Just try the head and see how you
feel.* According to the diagram on the package, that alien robot
head contained five milligrams of medicinal THC, and how I felt
after tearing off and eating it was . . . extremely high. Not high
like my bad teen experiences; not thick, paranoid, or immobilized, but pleasantly high; relaxed, at ease, smiling, light as
a feather. The following morning, I experienced the slightest
grogginess but no real hangover, no detectable ill effects. A
beautiful friendship was born. And that's how I became a pothead in my late forties.

I consumed part of the alien's body every night, and after it
was gone I sought other sources for THC gummies. Recreational
cannabis was not yet legal in Illinois, but this sure didn't feel like

a crime. It felt, in fact, like medicine, an antidote to my relentless, overworked life. I worked full-time as an academic advisor with two overloads: one as faculty-in-residence, living on the Northwestern University campus, offering weekly programming for three hundred undergraduate students; the other as a part-time lecturer teaching evening classes. I was also relaunching my career as a drummer, writing freelance, promoting my first book, and parenting a teenage son. I barreled through my days in perpetual overdrive. Too yang. The low dose of cannabis softened me, yinnized me, shepherded me.

How Do I Love Thee?

THERE IS A magic to weed: it brings a glow, a brightening of perception, an openness to experience, an ease of being. It turns down the volume on my fears and worries about my children, my anger about the social and political state of the world, my stress and exhaustion from work, and the prolonged uncertainty and loss wrought by Covid-19. It helps me sleep, makes listening to music or watching television more fun, soothes my aching joints, shakes up my dull, repetitive patterns of thought.

I'm going to do high yoga, I announce to Jake, before my nightly routine of gentle yoga. I feel a delicious wonder, flowing through the simplest stretches and movements. Hugging my knees into my chest is profound; lower back lengthens, sacroiliac joint settles back into alignment with a gentle thunk. I sink into the sensations, surrender to gravity. *I mean have you ever really FELT gravity?* It's like when I first practiced yoga in my twenties, amazing, a revelation to feel my face relax and open, my shoulders drop, my breath deepen. Over the decades

I'd grown habituated to the practice, less conscious. I never stopped loving yoga, never stopped benefitting from it, but I hadn't freaked out over it in a long time, until high yoga, which made it new again.

And high sex. Sex had been a great pleasure in my younger adulthood, but menopause changed my body, as it does, and left me drier, less desirous. Cannabis is a fix, takes me out of my head and deep into the warmth of my body, helps me rediscover a sense of surrender. High sex is not acrobatic; it's slow, attentive, responsive. My skin becomes extra sensitive, every brush of fingertips electric. And climaxing is like Nigel Tufnel's special amp in *This Is Spinal Tap*: these orgasms go to eleven.

Other things, too: A high hot bath, utterly dreamy; the water has presence, texture, agency, silk on my skin, heat reaching into the center of my muscles; *let go*, says the water, and I comply, exhaling, melting. A high cup of spearmint tea, total delight; the flavor intensified, an entire field of spearmint on a sunny day distilled into each sip.

I become a better, more enlightened version of myself on cannabis: more aware, appreciative, insightful, open. It makes me wonder. Does THC correct some chemical lack in my brain? Might I be . . . weed deficient?

Weed Deficient

"WEED DEFICIENT" IS a real thing. Kind of. Only it's called endo-cannabinoid deficiency syndrome. We are all born with an endocannabinoid system, a complex cell signaling system in our bodies, comprised of receptors (sometimes referred to as "locks") and chemical compounds that bind to them ("keys"). THC, the psychoactive compound in cannabis, is one of the keys that binds to our endocannabinoid locks, but our bodies also naturally manufacture internal keys, including one with the beautiful name "anandamide" (*ananda* means "bliss" in Sanskrit). In *Cannabis Is Medicine*, Bonni Goldstein, MD, writes that the endocannabinoid system regulates "gastrointestinal activity, cardiovascular activity, pain perception, maintenance of bone mass, protection of neurons, hormone regulation, metabolism control, immune function, inflammatory reactions, inhibition of tumor cells." It does this by regulating "the flow of chemical messages that are sent between cells, with the goal of maintaining homeostasis."[48] When we suffer from illness, infection, injury, or stress, the endocannabinoid system kicks in to bring us back into cellular balance. Our cells will manufacture extra internal keys, like anandamide. But what if the endocannabinoid system isn't functioning well and doesn't create enough keys to fit the locks?

Doctor Goldstein writes that "deficiency of endocanna-binoids can lead to anxiety and depression, eating disorders, fibromyalgia, Parkinson's, migraines, and more."[49]

So what can we do about it, doc? "The cannabis plant contains a 'treasure trove' of compounds that interact with the endocannabinoid system, helping to restore balance to the cellular messages."[50]

I have decided, with admittedly zero evidence and little more than a stoner's hunch, that my regular edible consumption has been an effective practice of self-medication for endocannabinoid deficiency. Self-diagnosis: I am weed deficient.

What Comes from the Dirt

ACCORDING TO RONALD K. Siegel, a pharmacologist who has studied intoxication in animals, it is common for animals to deliberately experiment with plant toxins; when an intoxicant is found, the animal will return to the source repeatedly, sometimes with disastrous consequences. Cattle will develop a taste for locoweed that can prove fatal; bighorn sheep will grind their teeth to useless nubs scraping a hallucinogenic lichen off ledge rock.[51]

—Michael Pollan, *The Botany of Desire*

Dude, Where's My Car?

IN HIS MAGNIFICENT 2001 book, *The Botany of Desire,* Michael Pollan postulates that our deep relationship with cannabis is partly attributable to one of the plant's specific effects on our brains: cannabis scuttles our ability to remember, causing short-term memory loss. Maybe that doesn't sound advantageous, admits Pollan, but think about it. "Much," he writes, "depends on forgetting."[52]

He argues that our mental health, our very sanity, "depends on a mechanism for editing the moment-by-moment ocean of sensory data flowing into our consciousness down to a manageable trickle of the noticed and remembered."[53]

Some amount of forgetting is necessary. But there's more: "Memory is the enemy of wonder," declares Pollan, "which abides nowhere else but in the present."[54] When we are high and forgetful, we are "draining the pool of sense impression as quickly as it fills,"[55] which has the result of focusing and intensifying our sense impressions and giving us that distinctly pothead "aura of profundity."[56] Time slows, even stops, and without our ordinary orientation to time, there's nowhere to be but in the present, an experience that normally eludes us.

"Banality depends on memory,"[57] concludes Pollan. The awe and wonder we feel when we're high—high yoga, high sex, high spearmint tea—resides "at the very heart of the human desire to change consciousness."[58]

Awe and wonder and the great expanse of the eternal *now* are all perfectly described in this beloved William Blake quatrain, which I know is overquoted but is worth looking at afresh (a.k.a. high):

> To see a World in a Grain of Sand
> And a Heaven in a Wild Flower
> Hold Infinity in the palm of your hand
> And Eternity in an hour[59]

The Zipless High

So why did I give up cannabis? If it was truly medicinal and helpful, if it didn't cause any ill effects, if it was an intoxicating analog to the zipless fuck of Isadora Wing's dreams[60]—effortless, simple, consequence-free—then why stop?

As with alcohol and sugar, my cannabis consumption had become habitual; I wasn't making a daily conscious decision to get high. I popped a gummy mindlessly, every night. If cannabis previously kicked me out of a rut, it had now dug me a new one. I wanted to bust out of all these deep grooves. And I was a little afraid that it was making me dumb—not just temporarily, when I was high and blissfully forgetful, but all the time. Was pot shrinking my hippocampus, permanently rewiring my nervous system? I read conflicting research, but the consensus was that at the dosages I was using and the age I started using it, it was safe. Some studies suggest that THC can cause permanent damage with adolescent usage, or with very heavy daily use. But the damage may not be permanent. Other studies suggest that if there is cognitive damage, it could be undone after thirty days of abstinence.[61] The research on all this is sadly scant, though. Cannabis is still a federally illegal, "Schedule I" drug, meaning that the Drug Enforcement Agency has decided it—along with heroin and LSD—has "no currently accepted medical use and a high potential for abuse." Which is absurd, considering the number of doctors who prescribe cannabis to ameliorate the effects of chemotherapy, mitigate symptoms of post-traumatic stress, or ease the pain of multiple sclerosis, among many other uses.

Someday we'll know a lot more about this amazing plant. For my purposes now, I turned to some good old-fashioned me-search. I'd increased my dosage from five milligrams to ten, and the slight morning-after fog of my early gummy days began to thicken and expand. I was late to work. I forgot my passwords. And on the rare night when I skipped my dose, I struggled to fall asleep. Was this addiction? If so, it was mild, but I was clearly dependent. It bothered me: maybe I'd become too cavalier about using a psychoactive drug every night.

Dignified and Old

THERE'S ANOTHER ELEMENT to all these quitting experiments. I was testing myself, testing my strength, attempting to prove to myself that I had it in me to transform the chaos of my being into something ordered and dignified.

Many of the children of my generation, raised in the 1970s, grew up with boomer parents who valued freedom and looseness more than order and dignity. They attempted to carry their countercultural values into family life. They divorced, experimented with open marriages, smoked pot in front of their kids, and we, in turn, enjoyed the autonomy and leniency that they were denied as youngsters.[62] Not everything about this was bad for us, and I try not to judge these hippie parents, especially now that I'm a parent. We all do our best. In my younger years though, I harbored judgment, and like a lot of my peers I vowed to raise my kids with more stability and safety. Maybe even dignity.

For me, the anthem for this attitude is the song "Dignified

and Old," recorded by the Modern Lovers in 1976. The song is offered as Jonathan Richman's sage advice for the drama and heartbreak of youth: wait it out, Jonathan says, stay alive. Jonathan is lonely and dejected and mourns the loss of a girlfriend but sings that he won't die; someday he'll be "dignified and old." After making this promise to himself, he entreats the listener: "Hey kids," he calls out poignantly, asking us to join him in imagining a dignified future.

The song assures us that there's something to look forward to in aging. It's the opposite of '60s rock soundbites like "hope I die before I get old" and "don't trust anyone over thirty." This counter-countercultural ethos permeates Jonathan Richman's songwriting and is one of the reasons he became a touchstone for '70s punk and post-punk. In "Old World," he acknowledges that the old world is gone but insists he wants to keep his place in it. In "I'm Straight," he sneers at his romantic nemesis, "Hippie Johnny," who is "always stoned" and "never straight." I think there are deep psychological reasons for Gen X's love of Jonathan Richman. We're not the hippies that our parents were.

One delightfully overdrawn example of a Gen X young adult is Saffron, the bitter, straitlaced daughter on the U.K. sitcom *Absolutely Fabulous*. Saffron finds herself forced to act like a responsible parent to her hash-smoking, vodka-swilling mother, Edina, and her even more decadent wreck of a friend, Patsy. I was a big fan of *Ab Fab* when it first aired in the U.S. in 1994, the same year my first child was born. I identified with

Saffron. There were times when I'd felt her brand of sour disdain for the goings on of the adults in my life, when I'd experienced the kind of role reversal she enacts, forced to be the responsible one. Saffron's mother parties her way around London, trying desperately to stay relevant and appear younger than her age. Edina and Patsy are not presented as admirable at all—they are selfish and irresponsible. But I also found them, well . . . fabulous, and I couldn't help but identify with them a little too. I was a mom: I was also a rock drummer. I wanted to be strong and steady for my family, but deep in my heart I doubted that my wild years were entirely over.

I'm guessing we all have these kinds of dichotomous debates. Had I clung too long, even subconsciously, to a vision of aging as exemplified by Edina and Patsy? Was I, in middle age, more Hippie Johnny than I wanted to be?

Bong Appétit

In 2022, 49 percent of adults in the U.S. had tried marijuana—the highest percentage on record. In 2015, that number was 40 percent.[63]

Eighty-eight percent of Americans think weed should be legal. In 1969, it was 12 percent.[64]

Half of all cannabis users have increased their consumption since the Covid pandemic first put us on house arrest in March 2020. Sales to women have increased the most since then.[65]

In my local independent bookstore, there's a cannabis section, books of witchy weed spells, medical marijuana advice, and gourmet cookbooks, like *Bong Appétit: Mastering the Art of Cooking with Weed*. The publisher's blurb says it's "the *Joy of Cooking* for a new generation."

Weed is having a moment; everyone loves it.

Well, not everyone. Tucker Carlson doesn't. On July 4, 2022, a young white man fired an automatic rifle into a Fourth of July parade in Highland Park, Illinois, near my home in Evanston, killing seven people and injuring dozens. While discussing the horrific slaughter two days later, Tucker Carlson neglected to mention the accessibility and glorification of guns and blamed, instead, video games, antidepressants, women who lecture men about white male privilege, and "government-endorsed weed; smoke some more, it's good for you."[66] I loathe Tucker Carlson, and vehemently disagree with every word out of his stupid, smug mouth. Still, his reactionary fearmonger-ing struck a nerve with me. Had I become too uncritical of weed, wholeheartedly accepting its benefits while neglecting to acknowledge its potential risks, especially to developing brains? And do we always, in America, have to believe that more is better? Is it always maxima over optima?

Without You

I GAVE UP my beloved gummies and lived five strange months completely THC-free. Withdrawal wasn't like it had been with booze or sugar: no sweaty, gross feeling, no overt physical symptoms at all. But I was different; my brain shifted and resettled. Instead of waking in a fog, I woke in a quiet state of calm. Thoughts lucid, passwords recalled. The most striking effect was the explosion in my oneiric life; suddenly my dreams grew vivid, technicolor, and extensive; I spent way more time dreaming and awakened feeling slightly dizzy, trying to recall and process the wild, trippy party in my unconscious. Turns out this is a common occurrence when quitting pot—THC decreases the amount of time we spend in the REM stage of sleep, which is when we do most of our dreaming.[67] It's also when we cement new bits of memory and process emotions. THC users who quit like I did report the same kind of dream flood.

A weird contrast: colorful explosions during sleep, quiet

calm when awake. That calm easily slipped into a kind of drab grayness. I missed the warm glow. After a month, I was steadier, which bore out what I'd read about the thirty days it takes to undo the effects of cannabis on our brains. I learned to live without—I liked being able to read before bed, with a clear head. Waking in the morning was easier; falling asleep at night, however, proved challenging. I tried various strategies: extra chamomile tea, a lavender oil foot massage. These worked OK. I figured out sex (extra foreplay, extra lube). I gained some inner strength and self-reliance, giving up something I loved, successfully proving to myself that I could live without. But I never for one single day of those 150 days stopped missing it. I felt what Michael Pollan described as the "gravitational force" of the "magic plants." I could live without, but I never stopped wondering if life was better with. Is there value, as Pollan decides, in at least occasionally "letting nature have her way with us"?[68]

Angels or Animals

POLLAN WRITES THAT even the Dionysian Greeks knew that intoxication "was not something to be undertaken lightly or too often." It was "a carefully circumscribed ritual for them, never a way to live, because they understood that Dionysus can make angels of us or animals. It all depends."[69]

I talked to a friend about my daily use, and she confessed to taking a small dose of Valium every day. Her doctor says she has, essentially, a shortage of Valium in her brain. We agreed that maybe we all need drugs to survive in this world.

Maybe. I think maybe.

Cannabis is holy to many—the Vedas describe cannabis as one of five sacred plants, with a guardian angel (a deva!) living in its leaves.[70] To Rastafarians, it is a sacrament, believed to bring healing, peace, and inner wisdom.[71] Humans have been evolving with this deva for over ten thousand years,[72] and our collective evolution is ongoing, as is my individual evolution. I would continue to search for my own personal sweet spot. Cannabis isn't the devil's weed, nor is it a risk-free miracle. There is no zipless high. There is no zipless anything.

Caffeine

Absorbing Suffering

I SAT ON the couch, listening to a podcast interview with Merrick Garland, who was talking about the Oklahoma City bombing in 1995. I had little memory of this—my first son was nine months old when it happened and I was in the haze of baby tending. Merrick Garland broke down crying, recalling the daycare center, the children who died. His cracked voice reached me, landed in my heart, made me cry, too. I was particularly sensitive at the time—I was cutting down on caffeine and the withdrawal was crazy, my delicate junky body freaking out.

My headache intensified. I grew dizzy; my throat tightened and I ran to the bathroom, knelt, puked, paused, contemplated my entire cup of morning tea. Or not entire, as it turned out: I puked some more. Those bathroom tile moments of reflection. What goes through your mind when you're on the floor of the room you are not supposed to be on the floor of? You're only there when things are bad.

I thought of my friend Faith, who was in the middle of chemotherapy treatment. I'd seen her on Zoom the night before; she was finally out of the hospital, back at home. She said she thought chemo would be like the worst hangover you ever had. The kind where you feel you'll surely die, and that death would be a blessing. She thought it would be like that. But it wasn't, she said. It was much, much worse.

I'd emailed her to say it was good to see you and I'm thinking about you and I love you and she wrote back to say I'm back in the hospital. I can't keep any food down.

Years ago, I sent Faith a book by Buddhist teacher Pema Chödrön. Faith, being a better person that I, took Chödrön's teaching to heart in a way that I was never good enough to manage. There was one meditation about absorbing the suffering of others. You breathe in someone else's pain and imagine it being transformed by the light and compassion in your heart. You don't run away from pain. That doesn't help anybody.

That's what I thought about, on the floor of the bathroom. Something about absorbing suffering. Something about Merrick Garland and those children and their families. Later I cleaned up and made another cup of tea. But first I stayed a long time on the floor, my stomach clenching, my mouth bathed in acid, my heart aching with useless love. I wanted to stay there, feeling, breathing, not running away.

The Coffee Achievers

IT'S HARD TO imagine now, but there was a time in the late twentieth century when coffee wasn't a cool thing to drink; it was what old men drank. Cool kids drank Coke. There were exactly four Starbucks in existence, all in Seattle (there are thirty-two thousand today), and coffee consumption in the U.S. had been in decline for two decades when the National Coffee Association launched an advertising campaign called "Join the Coffee Achievers." It was 1983. The television ads targeted eighteen-to-thirty-four-year-olds and featured artists like David Bowie, Jane Curtin, Joe Jackson, and Kurt Vonnegut. The theme song was ELO's "Hold On Tight." The artists strut with guitars, fuss over a studio soundboard, or peer up from a typewriter while the song thumps and a bright voice narrates: *You are the new American society—the movers and the shakers—you are the new coffee generation. . . . Coffee gives you the time to dream it—then you're ready to do it. . . . Join the coffee achievers.*[73]

I was sixteen; I liked Bowie, Jackson, and Curtin, and I worshipped Vonnegut, who almost single-handedly redeemed my home state of Indiana. But my friends and I already drank coffee; the fact that it was what old men drank added to the appeal. We wore vintage dresses and fishnet stockings and frequented the charming old diners and cafes in downtown Bloomington. The coffee buzz was cheap fun. We spent hours in sticky vinyl booths sharing plates of fries and swilling free refills, sometimes drinking ten cups of the watery stuff. I didn't want to be a victim of marketing. I wanted to be punk, impervious to corporate influence. But those commercials had my number. My friends and I would sometimes refer to ourselves (with a sliver of derisive irony) as *coffee achievers*.

My coffee worship reached back to early childhood, when I admired the way my grandmother sat at her Formica kitchen table, so graceful and composed in a clean housedress, with a cup of coffee in hand, day or night. She served me my first "coffee"—a touch of Sanka with a lot of milk and sugar. I felt special and big, a wise child with the soul of an old man, and I loved its taste and smell.

Throughout my childhood, I aspired to one day be a grown-up coffee drinker. In my teen years I became one, but as an adult I've felt continually conflicted about my caffeine consumption and have expended a weird amount of energy trying to break free of the habit, with no lasting success. In my mid-twenties I switched from coffee to tea, a move originally intended to help me gradually wean myself off caffeine entirely. It didn't work that time. Or any of the countless subsequent times I tried. I managed to wrestle free once or twice, but only briefly, and I always fell back into the habit. Each time I quit was harder than the last. This time the stakes felt higher. This time my body had begun to scream at me, loudly: it had had enough. I'd become hypersensitive to caffeine and developed a host of alarming symptoms of caffeine overuse, like high blood pressure, intense heart palpitations, a severe bladder condition (which awakened me more than ten times a night to pee) and constantly twitching eyes (which made me look and feel pretty scary). I battled with insomnia and fell into a vicious cycle of relying on tea to help me recover from the bad sleep that was caused by tea. Four hundred milligrams of caffeine is considered a safe amount to consume daily, and for decades I'd hovered around that dosage with no serious consequences. Something changed, and I was experiencing consequences—perhaps as an effect of aging, or menopause, or even the stress of the pandemic. Bodies change. Mine was making demands.

Of all the things I quit in this quitting experiment, caffeine was the hardest. It's the only drug to which I was truly, madly, deeply addicted.

Junky

HERE I WAS again on the floor of the bathroom, retching. My head was a nightmarish cartoon head, expanding and contracting. My vision blurred—was I crying? Everything hurt, throbbed, ached, like the worst flu ever, deep pain, untouched by the ibuprofen swirling down the toilet. My brain decided to revisit a series of dark, low moments in my life. That time I stole money from a girl's purse at a party when I was eighteen. She accused me and I lied—she believed me, apologized. The friend I lost who wrote five unanswered letters before she finally gave up. The time I snapped at my son and he cried for an hour. The boyfriend I cheated on with his brother. That stricken look on his face. Regret flooded over me unregulated, out of control. I couldn't believe that caffeine had been the barricade between me and this haunted hell.

It reminded me of accounts I'd read of people kicking heroin in rehab. This wasn't that. This was me after I finally quit drinking four cups of tea a day. Fucking *tea*.

Much like the junkies I know, I'd organized my days around my fix. A heroin addict friend of mine told me about how when he was working as a touring musician, he'd need to plan several towns ahead, lining up dealers to ensure he could get the dope he needed just to remain functional. That sounded familiar to me. I needed 400 or so milligrams of caffeine a day to function, which I ingested in the form of four super-strong cups of tea—I used a big mug and two English breakfast teabags. (Maxima, maxima, maxima. One tea bag was not enough.) I had to get all the details right: the brand of tea, the length of brewing, the time of day. If I got it wrong—for example, if I had my first cup a little too late in the morning—I'd get a violent headache and never quite recover the day. Caffeine consumption of more than 100 milligrams a day tends to be habit-forming for most, but for some extremely sensitive freaks like me, any small variation in consumption throws the nervous system into chaos.

Caffeine is the most popular psychoactive drug in the world, and it's a clever drug; it doesn't exactly make you high. Instead, it makes you alert, focused, upbeat. It increases adrenaline, serotonin, and dopamine, and blocks adenosine, which slows down your brain as you prepare to sleep. It doesn't make you not tired, it just temporarily conceals your exhaustion. This particular "high" is an almost-universal state of being, a baseline consciousness.[74] Ninety percent of the world's adults use caffeine daily. When I told people I was off caffeine they didn't shrug like with sugar or get defensive like with booze.

They just looked at me with a worried frown, like I was a troubled misfit. To quit caffeine was to abandon normalcy, to enter a global minority.

It was also miserable. All the articles I read said to expect headaches for three days. That was a lie. A great big, fat, evil lie. I had a blinding headache and nausea for two weeks and then a milder headache for a further two weeks. It was a struggle to do literally anything—my muscles ached, my brain was a fuzzy mess of negativity. I'd never write again. Covid would never end. At the worst moments, life was joyless. I wasn't suicidal. I didn't have to kill myself. I was already dead. We all take this powerful drug like it's nothing. I wondered, repeatedly: *Why am I putting myself through this misery? Why not just keep drinking my damn tea?*

Seriously, what's wrong with being addicted to something if you have an affordable supply and it's not giving you cancer or destroying your life and relationships?[75] Our culture has a puritanical tendency to moralize addiction, to see it as a personal weakness. That isn't my issue. It's that it disturbs me to be owned by a molecule. I allowed myself to live dependent for most of my life, and now I wanted my eyes to stop twitching and my heart to not explode, but even more I wanted to be free to operate in the world without being addicted to any substances. And that's very hard for me to do, because—whether it's a quirk of my biochemistry or a product of my personality—I become addicted to things quite easily.

Mormons

On a lively Quora message board on the topic "Why do Mormons not drink tea or coffee?" Church member Chris Nash writes:

> This is based on the Word of Wisdom, found in Doctrine and Covenants 89, specifically D&C 89:9:
>
> "And again, hot drinks are not for the body or belly."
>
> When this commandment was revealed in 1833, the members asked what constituted "hot drinks." Clarification was given that specified it meant "coffee and tea."[76]

Jim Ashman adds:

> In general, although many Mormons drink soda with caffeine, the idea is to avoid habit-forming substances and stimulants. Some people are able

to partake of these substances without becoming addicted, but many people do become addicted to these and to many other substances, so the Word of Wisdom is a protection from these addictions and ultimately then provides greater freedom rather than being a restriction.

Religious studies scholar Robert Fuller suggests that the "Mormon ban on psychoactive substances was a strategy to emphasize difference from other existing religious groups."[77] A student of mine, a former Mormon, told me that the real reason Brigham Young established the no caffeine rule is that coffee and tea were expensive to import and impossible to cultivate in Utah, and he wanted the Mormon community to be self-sufficient.

I'd found some unlikely role models. I wanted greater freedom, I wanted to be self-sufficient. Maybe I also kind of liked being different.

My Five-Hour Energy Commercial Spec Script

PRODUCT: FIVE-HOUR ENERGY

TITLE: LATE-STAGE CAPITALISM

LENGTH: ENDLESS

VIDEO	AUDIO
1. **TIRED PEOPLE** SIT SLUMPED AND WILTED OVER THEIR OFFICE DESKS.	SOUND: Slow music (a children's lullaby)
2. A **HARRIED TEACHER**, FROWNING, HER HAIR FALLING OUT OF A MESSY BUN, IS SURROUNDED BY KIDS WAVING PAPERS AT HER.	ANNCR: (VO) Tired sucks.
3. A **TIRED MAN** TRIES TO MAKE A POT OF COFFEE, FUMBLES WITH THE FILTERS, WHICH FLY OUT OF HIS HAND TO HIS VISIBLE FRUSTRATION.	ANNCR: (VO) You're a busy person.

4. A **TIRED WOMAN** STOPS AT A COFFEE SHOP TO FIND A LONG LINE OF CUSTOMERS. SHE CHECKS HER WATCH. LOOKS UPSET.

    ANNCR: (VO) You don't have time for this shit.

5. A **TIRED MAN** DOWNS THE CONTENTS OF A SMALL PLASTIC BOTTLE. IT REMINDS YOU OF ALICE'S ADVENTURES IN WONDERLAND. HE'S A BEEFY GUY AND THE TINY BOTTLE LOOKS ABSURD. HE'S DRINKING 5-HOUR ENERGY: 200 MILLIGRAMS OF CAFFEINE AND A BUNCH OF BULLSHIT HERBS AND VITAMINS. IT HAS BEEN LINKED TO 13 DEATHS AND 92 ADVERSE EFFECTS AND IS BEING INVESTIGATED BY THE FDA BUT THE PRODUCT KEEPS SELLING AND THEY KEEP CRANKING OUT THESE INSANE COMMERCIALS.

    SOUND: Sparkling happy music

6. **TIRED MAN** IS NO LONGER TIRED. HE SMILES. HE WORKS ALL DAY IN A FACTORY AND THEN GOES TO NIGHT SCHOOL WHERE HE'S PURSUING AN ACCOUNTING DEGREE AND THEN GOES HOME AND DOES HOMEWORK BEFORE SLEEPING FOR 3 HOURS.

    ANNCR: (VO) 5-Hour Energy fixes tired. One shot, back to work, problem solved.

It's a tragic, late-stage capitalism version of "The Coffee Achievers." We no longer have time to grind beans, boil water, sit down, and take a break or a breath. We no longer have time to go to a café and do nothing for a little while, sip a cup of tea, stare out the window, chat with a friend, doodle in a notebook. Caffeine and the minute hand on clocks appeared roughly simultaneously in Western culture,[78] and it was only a matter of time before this drug would free us entirely from our circadian rhythms, enabling us to override human biology and our connection to the cycles of the sun.

Get your fix and get your ass to work.

Apollo and Dionysius

MANY OF THE books I've turned to for this project refer to "Apollonian" versus "Dionysian" aspects of human culture. It's an overused concept, but it's also a helpful juxtaposition, so I'll engage it briefly here. Apollo is the god of the sun, of rationality and order. Dionysius is the god of wine, dance, passion, and chaos. Michael Pollan writes, "If alcohol fuels our Dionysian tendencies, caffeine nurtures the Apollonian."[79]

Booze and caffeine had always maintained a complementary relationship in my life. A drink at the end of the day smoothed the edges of my caffeine-jangled nerves. A strong cup of tea the morning after wiped away any residual whiskey haze. With my experiment, I'd now stepped entirely out of the Dionysian/Apollonian cycle. I fueled and nurtured neither God. Who, then, did I serve? Is there a god of the dull and muzzy? A god of the in-between?

Google Search: Is There a Greek God of Moderation?

IT TOOK A month for the headaches to stop. Another month for my brain to function somewhat normally, allowing me to finish a complex thought or comprehend a challenging piece of prose. After abstaining for six months, I was mostly comfortable in my minority state of no caffeine. I was one of the 10 percent.

Sophrosyne was the personified spirit of moderation, self-control, temperance, restraint, and discretion. She was one of the good spirits to escape Pandora's box and abandon mankind in her flight back to Olympos.[80]

The ancient philosopher Demophilus allegedly said: "The vigor of the soul is Sophrosyne, the light of a soul free of disturbing passions."[81]

Sophrosyne had left me, left all of us, on this earth to fend with the unleashed contents of Pandora's box. When I was a teenager, I admired the straight-edge punks, while lacking the discipline to be one of them. I was still short on discipline, but I'd summoned more than I ever had. Maybe Sophrosyne was exerting some small influence on me from her home on Olympos. Or maybe it was punk god Ian MacKaye: *At least I can fucking think.*

Social Media

There Is No Forest

IF A TREE falls in the forest and there's no one there to hear it, does it make a sound? I always thought this question was a Zen kōan, an unanswerable question meant to awaken the novice meditator from habitual thought patterns into an enlightened state of fresh awareness. The most famous kōan, "What is the sound of one hand clapping?" originated in eighteenth-century Japan. I understand why I grouped these questions together in my mind—they are both about sound, and they both derail the brain from its well-worn tracks, but they come from different worlds. The tree falling in the forest is a sixteenth-century thought experiment attributed to George Berkeley, an Anglican bishop. And it has an actual answer.

When I close my eyes, I see Berkeley's hypothetical tree on repeat; I have an inexplicable connection to this tree, which might be why I'm particularly offended by its terrible overuse and abuse.

For example, a website for Northern Ontario businesses

asks: "If a company with hundreds of millions of dollars of business uses bribes to cement deals but no one heard of these niceties because the *Globe and Mail* did not write about it, did it actually happen?"

An acoustics and soundproofing company hauls out my tree to discuss the difference between sound and noise. Noise, they explain, is unwanted sound. The company promises to soundproof your business or home against the noise that a falling tree might make when it hits the ground.

A customer service coaching company takes wild liberties: "If you say you have a customer-centric culture, but you don't listen to your customers, are you kidding yourself? If a customer tells you about his experience but the right department doesn't hear about it, does it mean anything?"

And of course, there are jokes:

If a tree falls in the forest and no one is around to hear it, a hipster already has it on vinyl.

If a man speaks in the forest and there's no woman there to hear him, is he still wrong?

The question could be rephrased like this: Do things exist if they are not perceived? Bishop Berkeley argues that to be is to be perceived, and I guess he's also assuming there are no squirrels, birds, foxes, or fungi in the forest. If we accept all this, then the falling tree, with no one there to hear it, does not make a sound. In fact, there is no tree. There's not even a forest.

Me and 2,978 of My Closest Friends

ONE DAY I deactivated Twitter, Instagram, and Facebook. I didn't announce this with one of those posts about how I'm taking a break to be a better person, live a better life. I didn't know what to say, because I didn't know what I was doing or exactly why I was doing it.

I did know that I'd become lost in the online world. After a year of pandemic living, my normal social skills had evaporated, and my social media skills similarly slipped away. I'd never been a good Tweeter and I couldn't figure out how to work Instagram and Facebook anymore. It hadn't always been this way. In my earliest days on Insta, I delighted in posting videos of sizzling garlic and onion or inspiring snippets of live music. I loved arranging and photographing things: farmers market hauls, batches of cookies, stacks of books. Facebook occasionally made my life better, too: soon after we moved to Evanston, a new acquaintance invited me to join a Facebook group called "Aging Rockers of Evanston," and in that group

I met Becca, who became a friend in real life. By the end of 2020 though, my social media mojo was long gone. All I did was scroll, scroll, scroll, mindless, unengaged, looking for I don't know what. Sometimes I'd actually say, out loud, *what am I looking for?* What I found was emptiness, a shocking expanse of wasted hours, and a whole new kind of loneliness. Charming videos of a family band playing Beatles songs made me blue that I wasn't jamming with my kids. Why weren't we the kind of people who had a family band? What was wrong with us? Facebook fights about wearing masks to curb the spread of Covid left me despondent and hopeless for humanity. Fundraisers begging for money broke my heart. The noise was constant and overwhelming.

This Is Your Brain on Facebook

SOCIAL MEDIA WAS the fifth thing I quit. I knew withdrawal by now. Everything about social media is addictive, even the negative stuff: the unfavorable comparisons between other people's families and mine; the insecurity wrought by a pretty yoga instructor with toned arms. I was hooked by all of this. Even more powerful is the positive stuff, the hit of dopamine that lights me up when someone tags my band, posts a picture of my book, shares my photo of blueberry pie.

It's a myth though, that the rush we get from technology use is directly comparable to a drug high. In *Child Data Citizen*, Veronica Barassi explains that social media use increases dopamine release by 50–100 percent, while cocaine increases it by 350 percent. "People who claim that brain responses to technologies and drugs are similar are trying to liken the drip of a faucet to a waterfall."[82] But those drips have a special power, compelling us to return frequently for another little hit, and that frequency gives the platforms more of a chance to accumulate information about our lives and interests. The better they know us, the better armed they are to cater to our tastes. It's a different kind of addiction, a complex and nuanced relationship surpassing anything cocaine has to offer.

My brain had undoubtedly been rewired by hours on social media. I had a vague sense that the habit was damaging, and boy was I right. Research on social media effects shows that its use reduces attention span, impairs emotional and social intelligence, increases our sense of isolation, interferes with cognitive and brain development, and disrupts cycles of sleep.[83] I'd been worried that weed was damaging my brain—social media was a more likely culprit. You'd think that learning about all this would make it easy to quit, but it didn't; it was hard to let go. If alcohol represented looseness and cool; sugar, pleasure and delight; weed, magic; and caffeine, achievement and focus; social media was attention, validation, and sometimes even connection. It was a lot to give up, all that pain and pleasure.

I finally shook the Facebook monkey off my back, and the main thing I discovered when I straightened up and looked around was time. So much time. I hadn't realized how unconscious my habit had been—I'd drifted to Facebook when I was bored, aimless, or avoiding hard work. It was my prime means of procrastination, and without accomplishing a thing, sometimes without even engaging with a single post, an hour would disappear. Two hours. I've tended to think of time as something personal, something meaningful and valuable to me, something I seize or waste or lose track of on my own, but time transcends the individual; it is a key asset in capitalism and always has been. Barassi writes that the history of capitalism is defined by the practice of controlling people's "temporal behaviors." Industrialization couldn't have happened without clock time. Before the fourteenth century, time in Europe was organized around the movement of the sun in the sky, the turning seasons, and the accompanying rituals and festivals of the day and year. Clocks allowed institutions like factories and schools to use rewards and punishments to control workers and students. According to Marx, clock time organized and managed labor, and time regulation was fundamental to the assembly lines and productivity of Fordism. It's easy to focus on our own individual compulsion and addiction around social media, but in this current stage of capitalism—surveillance capitalism,[84] platform capitalism, whatever you want to call it—there are political and economic forces driving every online interaction. If nobody slows down and looks at your post, if nobody clicks or shares or writes or otherwise responds to it, it has no value. The tree has made no sound. Your data is the "new oil," and Facebook needs it, needs to store, process, and sell this data. And the acquisition of it requires your participation and time. Lots of time.

After I quit, days were longer and more open, I was less likely to wonder at night what the hell I'd done with an entire day. I continued to reach reflexively for my phone, but instead of staring into Instagram, I redirected myself to an article or essay. In the tiniest of revolutions, I'd won a battle against surveillance capitalism. I won back some time.

I also rediscovered my attention span. My ability to focus had been slowly eroding as I skipped mindlessly across the internet. Now it was a little easier to sustain intent, to finish reading what I started and not distractedly drift away.

I bought less stuff too, without those rabbit hole experiences of chasing a cute pair of boots to a commercial website. It was nice to take a break from that, the way that pair of boots follows me around, marching all over my Facebook feed forever until I finally relent and buy them.

And I found a healthy distance from the noise of the online world. This reminded me of being a kid, when sometimes I'd sit in a closet with a book, blanket, and flashlight: nowhere to be, nobody to answer to, oblivious to the machinations of culture.

Being off Facebook also reminded me of another childhood experience: I once ran away from home for a day, mad at my mom about something. When I came home that night, hungry for dinner, nobody had even noticed that I was gone. I thought they'd all be worried sick. Similarly, nobody noticed I was off Facebook, which reinforced what a nonentity I'd been there. I was OK with that—the world spins along without us, we are free to retreat. And was I really missing anything important?

No and yes. Friends played gigs, celebrated birthdays,

adopted puppies. Major shit was happening. Not only to other people but to me, too: my band celebrated the release of our CD after over a year of pandemic delay. I finished an MFA in Creative Nonfiction. Just like I was disoriented by not celebrating with alcohol, so too was it destabilizing to not share a happy Facebook post. With apologies to Bishop Berkeley: if a great thing happens, and you don't post about it on Facebook, did it really happen?

When my dear friend Faith Kleppinger—writer, musician, one of the best humans I've ever known—died a few days after her fiftieth birthday, I coped without posting about it. If a bad thing happens, and you don't post about it on Facebook, did it really happen?

I Am a Tree

FAITH'S SISTERS WERE by her side. Her whole family was with her. She did not fall alone. Unlike the tree in my mind's eye, which never stops falling and is always alone. Faith, I think I am a tree, falling. I am talking to you and you're not here, so I don't know if I am actually making a sound.

But

SOMETIMES BEING ALONE, and even falling alone, is exquisite.

This Is the Song That Doesn't End

I DIDN'T POST on Facebook about Faith, and she died in the middle of a pandemic. There was no chance to sit with her in hospice, no memorial to attend. I grieved on Zoom with a small group of friends. I tried to write a poem about her. I couldn't finish it. Here's what I got:

> This is a poem to my friend Faith
> Who said goodbye to me and shut the
> Book and left the world
> And left me wondering do I even know
> How to be a friend? If I could
> Neglect her crystal eyes her
> Wicked laugh her songs, like fallen
> Stars trapped on tape her voice
> The frequency of fairy queens and
> The way I sat in her heart. She
> Thought too much of me. I deserved

Less of her love,
And still.

I don't know. I can't finish it. I'm not a poet and I'm not good at endings: not as a writer, not as a drummer. Ask anyone who has ever played with me—I blow endings all the time. The drummer is supposed to be the authority, the driver in the band, but unless a song has a neat, clear ending, I tend to panic in the outro. Sometimes I just keep playing until everyone else stops, flashes me dirty looks, and the song falls to pieces, like the tree continually falling; endlessness is its own special hell. Remember *Lamb Chop's Play-Along*, that horrifying children's show on PBS with Shari Lewis and her lamb puppet? They'd end every show by singing "The Song That Doesn't End." A nightmare. Hamlet has the only true ending: everybody dies.

The Pose of the Corpse

I DON'T KNOW what it's like to be dead, but I imagine it's a lot like not being on Facebook. We have to practice dying, it's necessary. In *How We Live Is How We Die*, Buddhist nun Pema Chödrön observes that people who "open themselves to the inevitability of their death" are "more engaged in life and more appreciative of what they have."[85] One of the five foundational "remembrances" of Buddhism is "I am of the nature to die. There is no way to escape death."[86] Some Buddhists recite this every day. It seems like a good idea to me. Marcus Aurelius, Roman emperor and Stoic philosopher, wrote in his *Meditations* that "you may leave this life at any moment: have this possibility in your mind in all that you do or say or think."[87] I'm not Buddhist or Stoic, so I practiced dying by kicking myself off social media for a while, standing in a soundless forest, as lost as ever, but perhaps the slightest bit more open and aware.

Everything

Straight-Edge Summer

AMERICANS COLLECTIVELY CAREENED into summer 2021, optimistically dubbing it "hot vax summer." Or "hot girl summer." And then a bunch of vaccinated people tested positive for Covid, and the Delta variant spread, unstoppable, and it became something else. Bullshit summer.

For me, it was straight-edge summer. I'd worked my way through my list of things to quit and sweated them all out of my system and here I was, straight-edge at last. I liked the simplicity, lightness, and freedom of it, all of which arose from making significantly fewer decisions in the day: should I hop on Facebook for a while to see what's up? Should I risk my bedtime with a late afternoon cup of tea? Should I surrender to this craving and bake a batch of cookies? Should I have a beer or a cannabis gummy tonight? No, no, no, no. Simple. Making decisions is exhausting; making fewer of them frees up mental energy. That's why Steve Jobs wore the same thing every day.

If before I'd felt overly defined by my habits and addictions—who was I, if not a coffee achiever, a pothead, a lush; who was I without my 2,978 social media friends?—now I was defined by all that I denied myself. I teach a class at Northwestern about food and culture, and in one unit called "You are what you (don't) eat," we talk about the characteristics of abstinence and groups who partially define themselves by what they avoid: vegans, Kosher Jews who don't eat catfish or pork, Muslims who fast during Ramadan. Abstaining from anything for a meaningful reason can strengthen your sense of identity in a group or as an individual. I'd felt this as a lifelong mostly-vegetarian, and I felt it now as an overage straight-edge punk.

I didn't only sit around abstaining. I kept in motion that summer. I finished writing my thesis. I read like crazy: fat, juicy novels like *Life After Life* by Kate Atkinson and *Hamnet* by Maggie O'Farrell; absorbing memoirs like *The Yellow House* by Sarah M. Broom and *Negative Space* by Lilly Dancyger; illuminating nonfiction like *How to Do Nothing: Resisting the Attention Economy* by Jenny Odell and *This Is Your Mind on Plants* by Michael Pollan. Instead of nursing a hangover with a mug of hot chocolate, I brought that hot chocolate (sugar-free, naturally) and a good book to bed, finding comfort, restoration, escape. Instead of lurking on Facebook and losing myself in the drama online, I picked up a book and lost myself in the drama of the story. I started writing and publishing book reviews. I dusted off my drumsticks, and after a sixteen-month hiatus, my Chicago band Sunshine Boys resumed playing gigs. We had cancelled our CD release show three times and finally, that summer, it happened.

It was disorienting to reenter public life, to stand in a room with two hundred people, to talk face-to-face, after months in a room with two, interacting with others through a screen, if at all. I struggled all night to finish a thought or sentence. And it was raw, hanging in a bar without the customary beer in hand, no anesthesia, nothing to temper my nervousness and anxiety. But it was a joy, too, to take the stage and pound the drums with my dear bandmates. At its best, drumming was primal, sweaty, like uninhibited dancing or sex, and it was deeply social, too, when everything was working right and I was able to drive and direct the songs and listen closely, responding and adjusting to the guitar, bass, and vocals. The connection that night was deep, and it reached the audience, who joined in, moving and smiling, an open celebration. Live music. I took it for granted before Covid. No more.

At one gig, later in the summer, a woman asked me what I was doing for my skin—a compliment. *No booze*, I said; she was disappointed, hoping for a skin cream recommendation. Truthfully, I'd hoped for much more of a visible physical transformation. Mostly I looked the same: mid-fifties, soft and saggy and faded. I'd lost a few pounds and my skin was clearer, but I'd fantasized that dropping all these habits would leave me glowing and youthful. Oh well. But I did have this nice, sweet sense of clarity, and a calm energy that I was grateful for after all the headaches, brain fog, puking, twitching eyelids, and erratic heartbeats. If I didn't exactly take a big, fat victory lap, I did at least feel quietly satisfied.

I'd done it. I'd quit everything.

My Own Private Prohibition

THERE'S A CATCHY Christian phrase about being "in the world" but not "of the world," which means that although we must live in this imperfect world, we must not become contaminated by its dark forces. It seems like a setup, a demand for purity and righteousness in this sea of sinners we're all swimming in. I mean, how's that working out for you, Christians?

Still, it's an appealing concept. The phrase doesn't exactly appear in the Bible but is extrapolated from a few verses, including these words from Jesus to his disciples on the eve of his crucifixion: "If you were of the world, the world would love its own. Yet because you are not of the world, but I chose you out of the world, therefore the world hates you."[88] And this, a prayer on their behalf: "I have given them your word and the world has hated them because they are not of the world, just as I am not of the world. . . ."[89]

I'm guessing these verses have brought comfort to believers who feel the tension between "the word" and "the world," and the loneliness that must ensue from this distinction.

During that straight-edge summer, as during the most stay-at-home part of the pandemic, I felt neither *in* nor *of* the world. I was camped out in my own private prohibition. As summer wound down and the end of my quitting experiment approached, I began to panic. This timing also aligned with my expected return to working in person at Northwestern after eighteen months of doing my advising job remotely. "Back to normal," people were saying, before correcting themselves: "the new normal." The new normal, the new normal, the new normal. I didn't want anything to do with it. I wanted to chain myself to my own private prohibition. I'd finally found a shred of clarity; I wasn't ready to reenter, not ready to be in or of. I'd worked hard to change; I'd come a long way. A surge of regret overtook me—I should have quit more things. I hadn't done enough. I should have quit dairy, biting my fingernails, using plastic, reading the news on my phone. I felt as despairing as a cokehead who's run out of cocaine. I needed more. I was addicted to quitting.

I Quit Quitting

I SAW THE 1973 film *Go Ask Alice* in seventh grade "health" class. Supposedly based on a real diary (it wasn't), the movie tells the story of an insecure fourteen-year-old girl who takes acid at a party and subsequently becomes a degenerate drug addict who meets with a cruel, sad end. That one acid trip was her undoing, like the teens in an even more ridiculous anti-drug film, *Reefer Madness* (1936), in which innocent high school students are tricked into smoking joints. Murder and mayhem follow.

It's all nonsense, yet in some irrational, middle-school corner of my mind I worried about un-quitting. Would my first beer in months set off a chain reaction of drunken self-destruction? Would I find myself gripped by the uncontrollable urge to eat a whole cake? Would I basically transform into a middle-aged lady version of Cheech and Chong?

Coveted

IT WAS NOTHING like *Go Ask Alice*. I didn't become a raving mad-woman.

I was at The Hideout, one of my favorite bars in Chicago, on a sweet, mild, late summer evening, calling for a charity bingo game with my Sunshine Boys pals, Jackie and Dag. In between calling numbers and handing out prizes and attempting goofy jokes, I sipped a beer, my first one in eight months. I'd been mentally drinking that beer—a cold, hoppy IPA—for weeks, watching in envy when people drank in my presence, to the point of wondering if all the craving and coveting was a sin against my commitment to quitting. A yogi friend of mine once said that if you crave meat, it's just as bad as eating meat; you might as well go ahead and eat it. When you become pure enough, good enough, it won't feel like discipline or denial to be vegetarian.

The beer lived up to my longing. I experienced a palpable release of mental pressure, right in my prefrontal cortex,

ahh. That old familiar relief. The goofy jokes flowed a little easier. Also palpable, though, as I headed into beer number two,
was my increasing slowness, fuzziness. At the end of that second beer, I found myself losing my train of thought, searching
fruitlessly for a word or name. By the very end of the night, I
was tired, but had trouble falling asleep. I'd become a serious
lightweight.

It's still the case now, a year later. I'm much more sensitive to alcohol, with a notably lower tolerance. I don't mind. I
drink far less than I did before my eight-month break, which
now feels like a true reset in terms of booze. I also joined the
dry January club this year. I almost never drink at home, and
when I go out I sometimes skip it—I'm learning to be out in the
world without a drink in my hand. It helps that nonalcoholic
beer has exponentially increased in tastiness, and most bars
offer craft mocktails. This makes it easier to fit in and helps me
avoid having to tell a big story about my strange and beautiful
dance with John BC.

I still believe in the benefits of imbibing (if you're not an
alcoholic or allergic or ill in a way that booze could worsen),
and, under the right circumstances, a cold beer is one of life's
great pleasures. I'm leery of my own potential smugness here.
I know I'll never reach some perfect state of equilibrium with
drinking. But this, I think, is kinda what optima feels like.

Inner Child

AFTER SEVEN MONTHS without sugar, I baked myself a small batch of brownies, sweetened generously with coconut sugar. I bit into one, still warm, and oh my god. I involuntarily moaned. I grinned. A rush of pleasure whooshed through my body, a wave of pure delight. The day's vicissitudes retreated, and I was a happy kid with a brownie in her mouth. The sugar deva showered me with joy and truly I was blessed. Sweet maxima. *Why*, I wondered, *would I deprive myself of this?*

Entropy

WEED. SIGH. IT didn't take me long to snap back to daily use. It's hard to imagine now how I even survived those months without. I've tried multiple experiments since my Big Quit—I stopped entirely again for a whole month, which was dreary, and then I tried repeatedly to abstain for three days every week. This seemed like the perfect compromise—four days on, three off. But I felt jumpy and didn't sleep well on those three nights off, while I tended to crash more easily on the nights I used. I found myself descending into disorder with every failed experiment.

Journal entry:

> Awful splitting headache, energy flatline. What is it that tilts me always to maxima? Unchecked, I'll always push to extreme. I didn't need to get high last night. I had a nice comfortable dose, six milligrams. I was fine, should have stayed

right there. I did an interview for a podcast and felt down; I wasn't articulate enough, fell back on my stale old talking points, forgot the names of people I should have remembered. I wanted to obliterate my dumb self, so I gobbled up an additional five milligram gummy, a particularly potent one, and two hours later I was spinning, tripping, miserable. I think that was the highest dose of edibles I've ever taken. Now I know how bad it feels to cross that line, and this might be my first terrible THC hangover.

I decided to quit things because, for one thing, I didn't like the idea of needing chemicals to make it through the day. Yet here I am, incapable of surviving one difficult night without weed.

Sophrosyne

I GRADUALLY ADDED back tiny, trace amounts of daily caffeine in the form of decaffeinated tea or coffee, and the occasional square of dark chocolate, consuming ten milligrams daily at the most. This maintenance dose is my version of methadone, and it's my deal for life. I will never, ever find the strength to quit again; withdrawal was too painful, too dragged out. Now my eyes don't tic, my blood pressure is lower, and my heart has settled significantly down. The sweetest thing, by far, is the freedom. No more planning my day around compulsive tea rituals. Like any real junkie, I'd had a long-standing fear of situations beyond my control. Traveling, for example, was a challenge: what if I couldn't find strong enough tea at the right time? What if I was abducted by extraterrestrials? They wouldn't necessarily be able to provide me with two teabags, four times a day, at steady increments of time. But hey, aliens— I'm ready for you now.

I Feel So Seen

I'M BACK ON social media. I resisted returning until well after I'd quit quitting everything else. I didn't have a plan, still, about how to be on social media—what did I want from it, what did I have to offer there? I got myself worked up, like there was a monster in the next room and I was certain that if I walked into the room the monster would eat me. So I crouched in hiding, wondering what to do. Maybe just take a peek? Or tiptoe quietly into the room? Maybe the monster wasn't hungry.

But haven't we all seen this movie? The monster is hungry. The monster is always hungry.

When I returned to my office, after eighteen months of working from home, I found my wall calendar, still on March 2020. It was very *Planet of the Apes*-esque, an undoubtedly Instagrammable image, and I felt a little empty as I took that old calendar down and hung a new one, turned to September 2021, sharing that moment of transition with nobody.

After a while I got tired of hiding and I popped back in one day, almost half a year after I'd popped out. I hover on the face of one of my 2,978 friends and say, *who the fuck are you? I don't know you. You don't know me.* Meanwhile, Facebook, the entity, knows me well. Paypal'd me three hundred and ninety-seven dollars, my share of the settlement in a class-action lawsuit. Knows I have heat-induced hives and suggests treatments and an upcoming drug study. Knows I'm in the market for a new summer dress. Knows I'm a permanent sucker for a beautiful vegetarian cookbook.

I feel so seen.

By which I mean I feel so surveilled. I am giving my data to a massive corporation and they are using it to sell me shit and make more money and for even more sinister purposes. *What is this three hundred and ninety-seven dollars for?* I asked a friend. *I guess that's the price of your soul*, he said.

All Hear

I EXPECTED QUITTING social media to be more revelatory. I thought that by stepping away I'd see my habit more clearly and find some answers to my questions: what am I looking for on Facebook? And what can I realistically expect from the experience? But I'm still lost. Maybe I'll figure out a way to make it work, to feel more connected and not less. All my life that's what I've wanted. It's what I wanted as a kid with the wrong clothes, wrong lunch, asking for the wrong books. It's what I wanted as a teenager, drinking beer to suppress my inhibitions enough to approach a stranger at a party. And it's what I wanted as a drummer, struggling but determined to lay it down, to lock in and merge with the band and audience, to feel the space between us all dissolve. Connection. It's never come easy.

There are some social media moments for which I feel an uncomplicated love: your cats and dogs and dinner and babies, your first day of school pics and your Record Store Day finds. Most days when I go on Facebook, I see a post about the death of someone's parent or friend, and these are always commented upon with expressions of sympathy and love. The post becomes a miniature, interactive art exhibit with photos, shared stories of the loved one, songs that you can click on and listen to, right there where you sit, hug emojis, heart emojis, crying emojis, offers of help: *message me if you want to talk. I've been through this too.* Has social media brought me more connection or less? I don't exactly know. And I know I promised an answer a while ago, but I don't know how to resolve the question about the tree, either: does it make a sound? Some theologians say the tree definitely *does* make a sound, but only to God. The tree falls: God hears. I'm agnostic; I don't know about God, but when God people have explained to me that they believe God is love, I've nodded my head sincerely. That resonates. I get it. Other God people have said that God is All, everything in sum. I think I get that, too. So we can translate— the tree falls: love hears. The tree falls: all hear. We're all here. And we all hear.

So What?

FOR MOST PEOPLE, drug use, dependency, addictive habits, it's all . . . fine. It's manageable. It's normal. It's nothing like *Go Ask Alice*. We are pretty much all hooked on something, many of us on multiple drugs, if you count sugar and caffeine, which I do. The question is, so what?

I have addictive tendencies, and I wonder how many of us are predisposed in this way. As a preteen, I was addicted to sugar, sometimes working my way through an entire package of Archway oatmeal chocolate chip cookies, one of the treats my healthy mother allowed in our home. I was often alone when I ate them, alone and hungry after school. Lonely. Cookies filled empty spaces in me. I wasn't only addicted to the sugar, but to the act of overeating, of going overboard. There were never enough cookies. There could never be enough. "Why is the rum always gone?" asks Captain Jack in *Pirates of the Caribbean*. Later came all the other things: caffeine, booze, cigarettes. Am I writing a book about addiction?

Am I writing a book about how I want to change, how I wanted the pandemic to give me the opportunity to radically change my life? It's crushing to find my life looking so similar to what it looked like pre-pandemic. My same old life, but with a mask on. That's not what I wanted.

It's My Wife and It's My Life

PERHAPS THE HEROIN had been there all along, waiting for us, but what it seemed like at the time—the late '80s—was that suddenly heroin was everywhere in Boston. I was there too, playing drums in the Blake Babies. In my circle of friends, heroin held an artistic, literary allure, equated with my favorite band, The Velvet Underground; junkie beat poet William Burroughs; and poet/rocker Jim Carroll, whose *Basketball Diaries* was canonical to us, and whose song "People Who Died" would soon become sadly germane. I maintained a naïve reverence towards heroin and junkies, along with a healthy fear of the drug—I figured it was something I'd never mess with; I wasn't cool enough, reckless enough. Then some close musician friends of mine began regularly snorting heroin and reported that it was incredible. It didn't take much convincing for me—no needles, the company and reassurance of good friends. I was in. Four of us camped out in a cozy Cambridge apartment one night; two in the group had experience, the others were newbies. I was warned that I'd feel nauseous and itchy and would likely vomit my first time. I didn't.

All I felt was this: perfect.

All sensations of desire and craving evaporated. Hunger, thirst, lust—gone. It was like some magical mechanism lifted every scrap of stress, fear, worry, and regret out of my being. I'd never felt this right: at home in my body, comfortable with myself. *This*, I thought, *is how I have always wished to feel. All my life.* We floated around together but separate for a few hours, a lazy, sweet kind of togetherness, draped across padded chairs, stretched out on blankets, listening to music—Brian Eno, John Coltrane. I closed my eyes and spiraled off into delightful inner visions; I saw myself onstage, singing Loretta Lynn songs. Singing is an activity that I've rarely done publicly, one that takes me to my most vulnerable and terrified place, but here I wasn't afraid, and the hardest thing in the world felt like the easiest thing in the world. After hours of blissful drifting, I collapsed into a deep, peaceful sleep. I was in love with a drug.

But I mostly stayed away from heroin after that night. I loved it too much, and my fear of it only increased after that one heavenly instance. I didn't trust myself to use heroin occasionally or moderately. I wanted to feel that way all the time, I wanted to live in that dreamy cloud with that serene sense of fulfillment. It had such an ultimate, zenith texture. That was danger. But a lot of my other friends kept using, and I didn't blame them. One night, out in a dance club with a group, Charlie moved in on me, talking close in my ear over Deee-Lite and En Vogue. He was wiry and feral, he worked in a record store with my boyfriend, and there was a flicker of chemistry between us. *I heard you tried H*, he said. Yes, I had, and I'd loved it. *You gotta shoot up*, he said, *it's like a million times better*. I was high from the music and dancing, breathless and sweaty, and this promise intrigued me. How could anything on earth be even better than what I'd experienced? I was interested. He wrote his name and phone number on a scrap of paper, and I pocketed it. Looked at it every day for a couple of weeks and fought with myself. I wanted to call. But I was terrified. Finally, I tossed it.

The Pursuit of Happiness

IN HIS 2021 book, *Drug Use for Grown-Ups*, Dr. Carl L. Hart argues that it's time to get real about drugs. I'm not the only one who likes to get high. Thirty-two million Americans, he writes, have used at least one recreational drug in the past month—and most of them are not addicts. He repeatedly invokes the Declaration of Independence and quotes the late ethnobotanist and pro-psychedelic drug mystic Terence McKenna: "If the words 'life, liberty, and the pursuit of happiness' don't include the right to experiment with your own consciousness, then the Declaration of Independence isn't worth the hemp it was written on."[90]

Dr. Hart introduces himself as "an unapologetic drug user" who is "a happier and better person because of them." He is a scientist and neuroscience professor at Columbia University and has worked for decades on issues of drug abuse and addiction. Only recently has he begun to talk openly about his personal drug use, which includes cannabis, heroin, psychedelics, and amphetamines. Hart upends multiple myths and stereotypes and assumptions, including the assumption that all "hard" drug users are addicts—in fact only 10–30 percent of heroin and methamphetamine users are addicted.[91] He expresses his frustration at the fact that he can talk comfortably in most social situations about his cannabis use but not his heroin use. And he argues convincingly for legalization and regulation of all drugs. In countries like Portugal, where drugs are decriminalized, there are not only fewer drug-induced deaths, but also fewer users overall.

By the time I left Boston in 1990, I had an expanding list of heroin-using friends. I agree with Dr. Hart that all drugs should be legal, and I agree that we all have a right to privacy and happiness. And I take Dr. Hart at his word that heroin isn't dangerous for him. I believe him when he writes that being department chair was much more detrimental to his health than his occasional drug use. But I don't share his casual stance on heroin. Of my small group of friends in Boston who started using at around the time of my first experiment, three died of overdoses within a few years. One landed in jail. Another was in and out of rehab and stole a friend's guitar to get drug money. One is still using, a committed "lifer" who only wears turtlenecks and long trousers to hide the track marks on her arms, legs, and neck. I don't advocate demonizing any drug or sensationalizing anybody's story. I think what I'm saying is I have a healthy respect for that drug. And I think what I'm also saying is: there but for the grace of God go I.

Hungry Ghosts

HUNGRY GHOSTS ARE demonic creatures found in all Far Eastern religions who are condemned to insatiable craving—thirst unquenched, hunger unfed, desire unsatisfied. Heroin was dangerous for me because nothing before it had ever silenced and settled the moans of my own personal hungry ghosts, nothing had ever quelled my incessant craving. Alcohol, at its best, had inched me in that direction, but it couldn't compare. It didn't come close. These days, I realize the value of craving, the necessity of dissatisfaction, how these forces have propelled me to every good thing in my life, from marriage to family to music to writing.

Heroin, in my limited experience, offered a tempting shortcut to happiness and satisfaction. It gave me everything I wanted, instantly. I suspected and feared that the price of everything would be . . . everything: health, happiness, life itself.

Il Est Interdit D'interdire

"IT IS FORBIDDEN to forbid" was a popular slogan in France during the May 1968 student protests. Playful, anarchistic slogans covered the walls:

"Insolence is the new arm of the revolution."

"Be realistic, demand the impossible."

I wrote "It is forbidden to forbid" on an index card and pinned it to my bulletin board, not long after I quit quitting. It looked lonely, so I added Holly Whitaker's 1968-worthy quip, "We need to create a life we don't need to escape."

Since when am I a person who pins inspirational sayings to her bulletin board? Rhetoric and motivational psychology were born out of witchcraft and magic. I was casting a spell on my bulletin board. A spell for quitting, for transformation, for my own little revolution.

Be Cool

ONE AFTERNOON, WALKING home from the grocery store, I spied an Evanston police officer, walking in the opposite direction. My shoulders tightened. A cop. Be cool. I arranged my face into its calmest, most neutral expression. Not smiling, not frowning. As we passed each other, I forced my eyes to look briefly into hers. I nodded casually, like how I thought a non-criminal person, someone with nothing to hide, would nod. Was she onto me? Was I busted?

But wait, I thought. I'm not breaking any laws. I'm a middle-aged white woman walking home from Whole Foods with a bag full of chickpeas and chard.

What is this book? Is this the tale of a midlife crisis?

Quitting as Hope for the Species

EARLIER, I REFERENCED Gregory Bateson's influential article about Alcoholics Anonymous and his concept of "optima" versus "maxima." Addiction intrigued Bateson, but his fascination was not so much with the drive towards addiction as with the drive to resist or break an addiction, to act against one's own comfort and happiness. It's like climbing a mountain, he says: halfway up the mountain and it hurts like hell, your feet are killing you, you're exhausted, it's horrible. The only logical thing to do is turn around and go home. Have some lunch. Yet most people carry on, take a deep breath, push through to the top.

We evolved to seek and covet the sugar buzz, the dopamine hit. There is nothing in our biological programming that pushes us to deny these things, to moderate our consumption, to decide we are better without—especially once we are fully acclimated and addicted. Heroin brought me bliss and contentment like nothing else; caffeine was a socially sanctioned jump-start for my brain; social media offered limitless distraction and entertainment. Yet some blend of fear and self-preservation moved me to refuse, to eliminate or moderate my consumption. It's a mystery, suggests Bateson. It should give us all some hope for the survival of our species.[92]

A Bluebird from a Paperclip

In 1966, John Martin founded Black Sparrow Press, primarily to publish the work of Charles Bukowski, whose poetry he'd read in an underground magazine. Bukowski had been working as a post office clerk for ten years. He hated the job, did nothing but the bare minimum required, picked up a six-pack after work and went home to drink and write. In 2022, people were calling this approach to work "soft quitting" or "quiet quitting." It's a kind of self-protective detachment, a declaration of limitations, boundaries. My job doesn't own me. Bukowski soft quit for years. And then he quit quit. John Martin offered him a stipend of one hundred dollars a month to leave his job and write full time. Two years later, Bukowski's novel *Post Office* was published. It sold a million copies.

Bukowski wrote to Martin about work and its devastation:

> And what hurts is the steadily diminishing humanity of those fighting to hold jobs they don't

want but fear the alternative worse. People simply empty out. They are bodies with fearful and obedient minds. The color leaves the eye. The voice becomes ugly. And the body. The hair. The fingernails. The shoes. Everything does.

He expresses his gratitude for escaping the grind:

So, the luck I finally had in getting out of those places, no matter how long it took, has given me a kind of joy, the jolly joy of the miracle. I now write from an old mind and an old body, long beyond the time when most men would ever think of continuing such a thing, but since I started so late I owe it to myself to continue, and when the words begin to falter and I must be helped up stairways and I can no longer tell a bluebird from a paperclip, I still feel that something in me is going to remember (no matter how far I'm gone) how I've come through the murder and the mess and the moil, to at least a generous way to die.

To not to have entirely wasted one's life seems to be a worthy accomplishment, if only for myself.[93]

I Changed the Name of This Town

I LOVED SINGER-SONGWRITER Lucinda Williams's self-titled album when it came out on Rough Trade in 1988 and I love it still. It explodes with genius, blends alternative country with blues and punk-y pop, tastefully produced to showcase her splendor as a singer and songwriter.

"Changed the Locks" is not musically the most inventive song on the album. It follows a standard blues structure and sounds at first listen like something you'd hear a dull bar band play. But it isn't that. It's a breakup song, addressing the erstwhile lover. The first verse declares a clean break: "I changed the lock on my front door." OK, we get that. The ex-lover has a key, but now it won't work, there's no ambiguity—he's out. He can't come inside her house. Things intensify in the second verse, "I changed the number on my phone/So you can't call me up at home/And you can't say those things to me/That make me fall down on my knees."

When's the last time someone made *you* fall down on your knees?

A couple of verses later, she slips into the extreme: "I changed the kind of clothes I wear/So you can't find me anywhere/And you can't spot me in a crowd/And you can't call my name out loud."

Now she's incognito, like a squealing ex-crook in witness protection, her very identity morphing, unrecognizable. She's quitting him by quitting herself.

And then this surreal turn: "I changed the tracks underneath the train/So you can't find me again/And you can't trace my path/And you can't hear my laugh."

The fucking tracks. Underneath the train.

Finally, the world is rewritten: "I changed the name of this town/So you can't follow me down/And you can't touch me like before/And you can't make me want you more."

Journal entry:

> I spent most of this year quitting things. I wanted to change, and I have changed, I've loosened the hold of habits and addictions, but I'm still myself: a bit lazy and unfocused, overwhelmed by all I want to do and am not doing, stuck in a full-time academic job I've wanted to leave for years. I quit everything and it feels suddenly like . . . nothing. Did I think that quitting everything was going to

make me a different person? A better person? Am I looking for freedom from myself, or freedom from the things that obscure my self? I've only changed the locks. What I wanted to do was change the name of this town.

Myrrha

IS THIS A self-help book? I'm not qualified to write a self-help book. I'm the least qualified person in the world to write a self-help book.

I can never remember my New Year's resolutions; I only remember my craving for a fresh start, for transformation. Real change, for once. Is it a fairy tale I want—godmother, glass slippers?

But what about the more troubling myths of transformation, like the story of Myrrha? She fell in love with her father, tricked him into impregnating her, and when he discovered the deception, she fled from his murderous wrath, begging the gods for mercy. The gods responded, finally, turning her into a tree. Her heartbroken tears became the resiny sap of the myrrh tree. She was safe from her father's sword, but still she must have longed for her pre-transformed state of imperfect humanity.

Is there a darkness in our longing for transformation, a secret wish to obliterate ourselves? Is wanting to quit the same as wanting to die?

The Limits of Moderation

THIS ISN'T ABOUT betterment. There is no best self, waiting to be discovered, uncovered. Let's call this an anti-self-help book. There is value, though, in questioning our ways and habits, and in embracing changing cycles of being. Habit can squeeze us into the tightest room, like the small, crappy apartment we were confined to for much of the pandemic. Living there was oppressive. It offered so few options for where to be, how to be, and I shrank to fit the space. Stuck. When we realized that it mattered a lot to have a home we loved, we found a new, pretty, expansive apartment, up in the treetops of Evanston. Life enlarged, became brighter. Unstuck.

Sophrosyne—temperance, moderation, prudence, self-control—can only take you so far. After all, she fled this world of chaos and confusion, leaving the rest of us to manage the whole catastrophe. My lifelong pursuit of an altered, improved identity is inextricable from my lifelong desire to make art—to act, drum, cook, write. All the relentless inner seeking for transcendence, connection, intoxication, and transformation has manifested in an outer drive to work and create. Restlessness and dissatisfaction are motivating, inspiring. They might even be prerequisites to creativity. I'm beginning to suspect that my attraction to extremes is not a thing about myself that needs fixing.

The Great Resignation

> SOME PEOPLE CHOOSE their precarity—evidence
> that precarity is not just a condition of our time,
> but a response to it. The precariat includes peo-
> ple who have forgone stable employment and
> retirement savings for temp work and travel
> and an uncertain future. Their very existence
> is unsettling, suggesting, as it does, that there
> might be something worth more than security.
> —EULA BISS, *Having and Being Had* [94]

It was mid-October 2021, I was sitting in my office on the
Northwestern University campus in Evanston, squeezing my
knees to my chest, poking around the internet, grimacing in
pain from a wicked UTI, bracing for a faculty mixer that I was
hosting, and mentally preparing to teach a three-hour evening
class immediately after. A *New York Times* headline leapt out
at me, and I clicked on the link to a video called "The Bravest
Thing You Can Do Is Quit."

The video recapped the story of gymnast Simone Biles, who withdrew from the summer Olympics that year, citing mental health issues. Commentators had dragged her mercilessly for being a "quitter." America hates quitters, glorifies grit and perseverance. Part of our issue is something called the "sunk cost fallacy," our tendency to keep doing something we'd be better off leaving, just because we've been doing it, have invested time and energy in it. This keeps us in bad relationships and unsatisfying jobs. Believing that you can't quit what you started is, declares the video, a trap. And this kind of thinking neglects to acknowledge another concept called "opportunity cost"—the price we pay for missing promising opportunities.

This video was talking straight at me. This video was reading my mind.

Powering through is often passive, says the narrator. *God this UTI is killing me*, I thought. *Ouch.*

*

THIS WAS MY tenth year as an academic advisor in the School of Communication, a job that almost entirely funded my MFA, connected me with hundreds of bright and energetic students, and provided a much-needed steady paycheck as I helped support my college-age kids. I'd cried tears of joy when I was offered the job, which had lifted me out of the precariat— before, I'd been temping and adjunct-ing, barely getting by. The advising job seemed perfect.

After a few years, I began to resent certain aspects of the

job. I missed having a more flexible, varied schedule, missed the freedom and agency I'd enjoyed as an adjunct. Many of my hours were spent in tedious administrative tasks that made me wonder: *for this I went to graduate school?* I didn't need a higher degree to enter data on a spreadsheet. Some days my sense of identity fractured: Wasn't I a drummer? An aspiring writer? What was I doing in this office? How did I get here? And although most of the kids were wonderful, some of them were, well, not. Some of them were entitled and snooty, and treated me like the help. There was an unpleasant, hierarchical structure at Northwestern that often got my back up, made me want to start kicking and resisting. But there was nobody I could kick, no means of resistance, so my bouts of anger and frustration ended in sad submission. What could I do? I needed the job. Maybe the best thing I could do was shrink to fit. I never hated being an advisor, I just grew less capable of taking and tolerating it all.

Covid was tremendously disruptive, bringing instant chaos and heartbreak, and loss on all levels. Every pleasure of college life was yanked away from the students as we switched to remote everything overnight. It was dismal, meeting on Zoom with sad, frustrated, stressed-out students, and I felt for them deeply as I struggled with a sense of helplessness—there was so little I could do to help. And of course, I had my own fear and sorrow and freakedoutedness to navigate.

But in terms of the rhythm of the days, Covid brought

immediate, radical benefits. I loved working from home. I loved the fluidity and flexibility of my schedule: I took walks in the middle of the day, napped or meditated after lunch, read more, wrote more. When my stepmother fell gravely ill, I relocated for several months to Indianapolis to help support her and my father—and barely missed a day of work.

I felt like I could breathe again; labor and life fell into balance.

After eighteen months, we returned to in-person work. On my first day back, I sat in a large, all-day meeting, masked to the gills, crying, practically hyperventilating, my heart pounding. I'd forgotten how to be out of the house and in public. I was also anxious, paranoid—people removed masks to eat and drink and I was certain I'd get Covid (I didn't). I didn't want to be there. I didn't want to be back. I had changed.

*

WHAT IF WE'VE been wrong about quitting? the video asks. *What if the bravest thing we can do is quit? As we emerge out of the pandemic, we have a moment to decide what we want our lives to look like moving forward. Embrace the clean slate.*

I swallowed all my UTI medication and hosted the reception and taught my class and crawled into bed at 9:45. I heard the narrator in my head: *Don't be a martyr to grit.*

*

I'VE NEVER MET her, but writer Eula Biss worked at Northwestern at the same time I did, teaching creative writing as a nontenure-track professor. Her work thrills me—her essay "The Pain Scale" is one of my favorites. Biss's most recent book, *Having and Being Had*, a series of vignettes exploring consumerism, labor, and capitalism, was inspired by the purchase of her first home. She meditates on precarity and the leap to middle class, on the ethics of investing and on structures of power, investigating the relationships between homeowner and house cleaner, husband and wife, employee and employer. What struck me the hardest, though, is her longing to leave her university teaching job. She feels trapped by a decent salary, the recent home purchase, and the fact that her job as a writer doesn't pay well. She tells a friend that she wants to quit her job—she'd still have plenty of work! She longs for time to write, and refers to Lewis Hyde, author of *The Gift: Creativity and the Artist in the Modern World*, in which he distinguishes work from labor. Work is hourly and rewards you with money. Labor moves at its own pace and rewards you with transformation. Biss describes small, painful power struggles at work: a senior male colleague infuriates her by aggressively dominating meetings, and then insists on a hug that only compounds her powerlessness and fury. She knows that others see her as "Professor," which carries weight and privilege, but she is a nontenure-track professor, and the difference means "the higher course load, the lower pay, the basement office, the glass ceiling."[95]

Powering through is often passive. I too was powering through. I'd been powering through for so long.

*

FINALLY, I DID it. I quit my job, giving my notice in the second half of 2021—along with twenty-five million other Americans. Anthony Klotz, a professor at University College London's School of Management, coined the term "Great Resignation." Other terms popped up: "quitagion," and the "Big Quit." The *New York Times Magazine* explored the trend in its issue titled "The Future of Work When No One Wants to Work." In an article with the headline "Seeking No Opportunities," Noreen Malone writes about a young editor she knows who was asked what her dream job was. "I don't dream of labor," was her tweeted reply. Anti-ambition was the cause célèbre. My favorite example is this viral tweet: "I hope this email doesn't find you. I hope you've escaped, that you're free."[96]

*

I HEARD RECENTLY that Eula Biss escaped; after fifteen years, she left Northwestern. She's free.

Book Lady

I LAUGHED AT that smart-ass tweet about not dreaming of labor. But we all must eat. When I worked at Harvard University as a low-level administrator, I was involved in the attempted unionization of the clerical and technical workers. The union made buttons to spread the word about the effort: "You can't eat prestige."

Sort of similarly, you can't eat tweets.

And we don't all have a John Martin at Black Sparrow Press to rescue us.

I was going to leave my job after the current academic year, but I still needed to work and earn money. I just wanted work that was a better match for me, something I could put my heart into. Something that would leave me with the time and energy to write.

I knew that I loved teaching; it was creative, challenging, inspiring. I especially loved working with the diverse adult learners in the School of Professional Studies. Adult education was where my heart was—I'd earned my undergraduate degree in my thirties at Indiana University's School of Continuing Studies, so I had plenty in common with these students. As I trudged through my long final year as an advisor, I was delighted to line up part-time teaching work with the school, and it looked like I'd be able to count on a couple of classes a year there. This was a major turning point; but it wasn't a living.

Books, I thought. Books are what I love, what had saved me during the pandemic, transporting me out of lockdown, across time and space, to 1970s California, 1950s Mexico, twelfth-century France. And writing—writing saved me too; sprawling stream of consciousness journaling that allowed me to examine my dreams, process my periods of withdrawal, and vent my frustration; or careful biographical writing that cast me as a detective, piecing together the details of a life through research; or succinct book reviews, that hurt my brain (in a good way) to create, distilling a four-hundred-page book down to a two-hundred-word review. How to combine books and writing and teaching and adult education, community education? Maybe I don't dream of labor, either. But if I could dream up a job and step into it, what would it be?

I emailed the owner of my favorite local bookstore, Bookends & Beginnings. *You should offer classes there*, I said. *I could teach some of them. And I could bring other people in to teach.*

The owner wrote back that she'd had the exact same idea,

years ago, and even had a name lined up for the initiative: Bookends University. She didn't have time to manage a new project, so the idea had lain fallow. It would be a solid part-time job with lots of freedom and flexibility. I could build the program, direct it, teach in it. Would I like to take a stab?

The Nest Will Be Full

AT A PARTY a decade ago, I made small talk with a woman a little older than me, a few years ahead on the parenting path. My oldest son, Jonah, was eighteen and had just left for college, and we debated the transition to adulthood—when does your kid become a grown-up? Was it the moment you dropped them off at college? College graduation? When they got a job and fully supported themselves?

I'll tell you when it is, she said. *It's when they get their own cell phone plan.*

*

AT ANOTHER PARTY, ten years later, I noticed I'd missed a call from Cecilia, Jonah's girlfriend. They had recently moved to Santa Fe together. Cecilia and I texted occasionally, but she'd never called me before. I jumped up to call her back. Jonah answered—his phone had broken, and he was at T-Mobile to replace it. And he thought while he was at it, he'd get his own cell phone plan. He needed me to release his phone number from our family account.

I felt a tad woozy. *Jonah!* I said. *This is it! You're an adult!*

I told him the story and he laughed. I freed up his phone number and passed it to him, my adult son. He had a college degree, a job for the Museum Foundation of New Mexico. He had health insurance, a driver's license, a wonderful girlfriend, and a cat named Dolly.

And his own cell phone plan.

*

JONAH'S YOUNGER BROTHER, Henry, was on a less straightforward path to adulthood, one that more closely resembled my crooked route. He had opted out of college to work on organic farms and make music, all of which slowed his full launch into the adult world. Still—Henry had a job and his own apartment, and whatever his idiosyncratic pace, he was moving into an independent future. The empty nest is a not a moment in time: it's an extended process.

*

BERNABÉ WILLIAMS FIGUEROA Jr. (Bernie Williams) played baseball for the New York Yankees from 1991 to 2006. He was a member of four championship teams, hit 287 home runs, and was a five-time All Star, among other stellar baseball achievements. He's also an extraordinarily talented guitarist who was nominated for a Latin Grammy.

He's also an exceedingly personable guy. I met Bernie at a benefit gig we were both playing, and while chatting with him backstage we made our way to the subject of grown kids and empty nests.

The thing is, said Bernie—*speaking from experience, the nest won't be empty. It'll be full.*

I smiled. I understood, abstractly, this sweet sentiment. But I didn't fully get it until now. The nest could be full. It could be full. Full.

I Quit Motherhood

THE POWERFUL LOVE I feel for my children is boundless, and obviously I'm still a mother and always will be. But I'm exiting the years when much of my time and energy has been occupied by the care and feeding of sons. The Triple Goddess is a neo-pagan archetype, with origins in Greek and Hindu mythology. The Goddess has three aspects: The Maiden, who represents the young blossoming woman, still a virgin; The Mother, a woman of childbearing and childrearing age; and the Crone, the wise old woman, post-menopausal.

"Crone" is not a positive word in our culture. At worst it connotes malevolence, the scary Halloween witch (Britannica defines crone as "a cruel and ugly old woman"), and at best a faded irrelevance, the sweet doddering grandmother. This is certainly worth resisting. In *Goddesses in Older Women: Archetypes in Women Over Fifty*, Jean Bolen compares the crone stage of life to "the fresh green of spring, where she welcomes new growth and possibilities in herself and others."[97] The crone years are a time of wisdom and responsibility. If we trace the etymology of the word back to the Old Dutch, we find that it comes from "corona," which means crown, or wreath. It might be hard to reclaim the crone from her cultural baggage, but many neopagans and others attempt to do just that, holding ritual "cronings" to celebrate the passage to this potentially liberating and transformative stage of life. I'm all for it. I've wondered, though, if we need a new word. Maybe something that links back to the word's regal roots in Old Dutch.

How about this for the three aspects of the Triple Goddess: Maiden/Mother/Queen?

Sir Elton John and I

In 2018, ELTON John announced that he would retire from the road after a lengthy tour, Farewell Yellow Brick Road, scheduled to end in 2020. This news caught my attention. I was recovering from back surgery after destroying most of one of my lumbar discs, the result of years of wear from the repetitive movement and torqued torso that drumming required, not to mention the abuse of lugging around all my heavy gear. I wondered if I'd reached the end of my drumming career. I was fifty-one. I'd had a good enough run.

In fact, I'd had a lucky, late-career bonus. After years of drumming in bands including Blake Babies, Antenna, Some Girls, Gentleman Caller, and Mysteries of Life, I'd taken a long time off, moved to England and back, gone to grad school, launched an academic career, and become a published writer. I assumed I'd quit music, but after a couple of years of living in Evanston, the closest suburb to Chicago, I gradually began to play again, doing one-off gigs with alt-country legend Robbie Fulks or Walter Salas-Humara from the Silos, booking the occasional Mysteries of Life show. It didn't add up to much, until I met guitarist/singer/songwriter Dag Juhlin and bass player Jackie Schimmel, both über-talented longtime veterans of the Chicago music scene. Dag's band, The Slugs, had shared a bill with Blake Babies in Chicago in 1990, and more recently he played guitar for Poi Dog Pondering and led a stellar cover band called Expo 76. Jackie played with kids' artist Justin Roberts and had been nominated for multiple Grammys. We started a band together called Sunshine Boys, the name a nod to the Neil Simon play about aging vaudevillians, still kicking.

It was 2016 and I was amazed to still be kicking, starting a brand-new band from scratch, thirty years after I'd started my first. It was improbable and impractical and most of all it was delightful, like finding love very late in life. We all knew better than to take it for granted.

Before Sunshine Boys, I'd nursed a sad, disappointed grudge against my drumming career. I'd been lucky, played in more than my fair share of good bands with ridiculously talented people, but I'd never fully pushed myself as a player and band member, never came close to what I imagined was my full potential. I was never going to be one of the great drummers. But I knew I could be better. The universe gave me one final chance, and I leapt at it. I've never worked as hard in a band as I did in Sunshine Boys. We practiced in a focused, collaborative way; we gigged often, and we recorded everything, releasing, in the end, two full-length albums and three singles, all among the best music I've ever created.

It could have all come crashing down when, two years in, I blew out my disc. Elton John had announced his retirement. My time was coming—but I wasn't there yet. Sir Elton had given himself a long final leg, two years. That sounded about right to me, and I figured I'd do the same. I just had another thought or two to complete on drums. Dag and Jackie helped me rig up a standing drum kit so I could resume rocking without reinjuring my back. We wrote and arranged a new batch of songs and recorded our second full-length album, *Work and Love*, a title that perfectly captured the spirit and values of our band. We planned to play as many shows as possible to promote *Work and Love* when it came out in the late spring of 2020—I'd be out there on my final gigs right as Elton John was doing the same.

Obviously Covid scuttled my and Sir Elton's plans. Would the long months of pandemic hiatus result in a change of heart? I did miss playing shows when I was stuck at home, but only a little. The time served to reinforce my knowing that it was time to wind down my drumming years. I'd already injured my back, and my joints were speaking to me too—wrists, elbows, shoulders, knees, all had suffered abuse, and I wanted to preserve their remaining function. *Baseball players don't play forever* is a thing I started to say to everyone I know. Those Covid months also found me with my nose in a book and a pen in my hand. I couldn't visualize myself playing drums at, say seventy, but I could see myself reading and writing, and wasn't it time to shift focus, to move into life's next chapter?

Soon after I gave my notice at work, I gave my notice to Dag and Jackie. I'd quit drumming countless times before. Now I was really, truly quitting.

But no—I stopped using the word "quitting." Sir Elton was "retiring." Retirement was something you earned, something intentional, something to celebrate. I wasn't stopping out of pain or exhaustion or fear or failure or circumstances beyond my control, although I'd contended with all those factors in my thirty-six-year career. This was different. Sunshine Boys had been an incredible gift, leaving me, finally, satisfied that I'd done my best, that I'd taken drumming as far as I was able. I could retire with a peaceful heart.

The final Sunshine Boys performance was the pinnacle of my musical career. I'd never brought so much of my soul and being to a show. I didn't pace myself, didn't save a single penny for later—I blew it all. We played two sets, covering almost our entire repertoire. I sat backstage at the end of the first set, looking at myself in the mirror, drenched in sweat, like I'd jumped into a swimming pool fully clothed. *This is it*, I said to my reflection. *No sleepwalking.* I pounded and rocked through the second set and by the end I wobbled visibly, struggling to stand up. For our encore, we played the Wings song "Let Me Roll It" and I sang the first verse, probably not in tune, but definitely with emotion. *I can't tell you how I feel*, I sang, to the audience, some of whom had traveled from Boston, St. Louis, Minneapolis, some of whom had been watching me drum for over thirty years; to people not in the room, who had inspired and nurtured my career, like Faith, who always loved my drumming, when all I could see were my weaknesses and limitations; to my band-mates, who had encouraged and lifted me more than they'd ever know; to myself, on the brink of a truly major life change. My heart was like a wheel and I sang it—rolled it—to all of us.

I couldn't have written a better conclusion to my drum-ming years. That show should have been my last gig. But it wasn't—I agreed to play a benefit concert a week later. *Wow, great one-week retirement, Cher*, teased a friend of mine. Elton John announced in 1977 that he was embarking on his final tour. Look, we all change our minds. It's hard to let go of some-thing that has defined you for decades. I first began to play music because I loved songs and bands and I wanted to live in the musical world. My happiest high school moments had been in theatrical productions. I never played the lead, was usually in the background as a dancer or member of the chorus, but I didn't need to be a star to be happy—it was about merging into a collective of close-knit eccentrics, creating something we believed in. Being in a band extended this quest for creative connection.

When my band Blake Babies enjoyed some success in Boston, I noticed that being a drummer also gave me status. It didn't matter that I wasn't great. Drumming was hip. I got a little hooked on that. It made it hard to give up later—why would anyone relinquish this kind of cultural capital? In recent years, when I met people at parties, I could see myself reflected in their eyes: an OK-looking middle-aged woman. Until they asked me what I did and I said, among other things, drummer. I got used to the change in expression to one of interest. *Wow*, people said. *Cool.* These exchanges gave me an easy self-assurance, but they irritated me too, made me feel both lazy—the way I leaned on that aspect of my identity—and also limited, boxed in. I'd quit drumming many times, always hoping to find new ways to define myself. I tended to go to extremes, thinking I had to erase that part of myself completely. During my longest hiatus, I deleted all traces of my musical past from my resume and bio. This time I tried a different approach, changing the line in my bio from "drummer" to "retired drummer." I like how it looks—dignified and celebratory. The word drummer is still there, still part of who I am. It always will be.

This Is the Book That Doesn't End

MY FINAL SHOW before retiring was Hot Stove Cool Music in Chicago, a benefit for a philanthropic organization called the Foundation to Be Named Later, a Chicago/Boston nonprofit. I loved the generous, collaborative spirit of Hot Stove, the way musicians mixed and matched, crammed onstage in ridiculous configurations (there were often FIVE guitarists on any given song), played originals and big crowd-pleasing covers, throwing themselves into a gig that didn't pay a dime. I played percussion for Eddie Vedder, partied with Theo Epstein, got marriage advice from Bernie Williams, and shared a bill with idols of mine, including Liz Phair and Mavis Staples. The concert happened twice a year, once in Boston and once in Chicago. The Boston show always included an assortment of Chicago musicians and vice versa, which made it feel something like rock and roll summer camp, every show a happy reunion. When I noticed, after my first Hot Stove, that there were a whole lot of guys onstage and way fewer women, I worked with Tanya

Donelly of Belly and the Throwing Muses and Kay Hanley of Letters to Cleo, along with a long list of other ass-kicking women,[98] to create Band of Their Own (BOTO), a Hot Stove all-lady supergroup. BOTO became a beloved part of the Hot Stove lineup. By the time I got to my final gig, I'd played at seven Hot Stoves, including one virtual event we put together during Covid.

Now here I was, for one last waltz. My former bandmate in the Blake Babies and Some Girls, Juliana Hatfield, shared the bill, and we'd agreed to play a couple of songs together. Talk about your full circles; I'd first played with Juliana in Boston when we were nineteen years old.

It was a momentous night that marked the end of a momentous week. I'd played my last Sunshine Boys show, finished my final days of academic advising. I was wrapping a big year and a half, months of quitting, withdrawal, and rearrangement. And I was wrapping monumental decades of youth, rock and roll, and the day-to-day demands of parenthood. That dumb F. Scott Fitzgerald quote about Americans not having second acts. That was wrong.

I'd had a second act. My heart was set on a third.

This part of the story—self-help book, midlife crisis, makeover, addiction narrative—whatever it was, it was building to a conclusion. The next morning, I'd wake up in a town with a new name, with two part-time jobs that suited my soul—one as a teacher in the School of Professional Studies, the other as programming director for the educational events in my dear local bookstore. I would soon have two books under contract and the word "retired" in front of "rock drummer" on my bio. One son had his own cell phone plan. The other son was surely on his way. I felt like a coffee achiever. A decaf coffee achiever.

*

I CAME TO Hot Stove ready to party, wearing a silver velvet dress that—by happy coincidence—matched the silver sparkle drum set onstage. It was a packed house, an exuberant night. I drummed with my Sunshine Boys bandmates to the Go-Go's infectious "Our Lips Are Sealed" with Kay Hanley killing it on lead vocals. I played two Some Girls songs with Juliana, accompanied by my friend and drumming mentor Gerald Dowd on percussion. For the finale, I joined Juliana's wonderful band for a double-drum-set jam on ELO's "Don't Bring Me Down." It had been a spontaneous sound-check decision to add me to that song and it sounded incredibly great at that run-through—it was hilarious and over-the-top to have the normal army of Hot Stove guitarists along with two drummers on full kit. It would be the last song I would perform at my last gig ever, and I loved the idea of closing this act on such a high note.

*

I'D COME A long way from the very beginning of my drumming career. My inaugural rock gig was with an extremely short-lived Bloomington, Indiana, band called Medium Cool, which included my boyfriend and fellow future Blake Baby John Strohm. We played at a party in a crusty old building on the south side of Bloomington's downtown square, a building that artists flopped in back in the '80s. They threw parties and hosted bands, and we talked them into letting us onto a bill. I'd been playing drums for two months and we'd learned covers by The Velvet Underground, The Dream Syndicate, The Violent Femmes. I was confident that we were ready to play in front of people, that I was ready to rock.

By the end of our first song, my tense, sweaty hands struggled to hold onto my drumsticks. In the middle of the second song, one of those sticks slipped out of my grip midair and flew across the room. There was nothing to do but stop playing, stand up, walk out into the crowd, which parted for me (I heard laughter but kept my eyes down), pick up the errant stick, and, while the band nearly collapsed, trying to keep the song going, shooting me angry looks (oh, the looks that drummers get), jump back in and finish the song. That was bad. Even worse: it happened again during the third song. In *The Bad News Bears*, the newly formed team of misfits forfeits their first game in abject shame, having given up twenty-six runs without a single out. That's what the Medium Cool gig felt like to me. Afterwards an older drummer who I admired said, *You guys sounded good, except for those times when you*—he paused, trying to find a diplomatic way to go on—*stopped*. It was humiliating, and I was crushed. I wouldn't play again until I'd moved to Boston, formed the Blake Babies, and regained my confidence.

*

AT HOT STOVE, the ELO song was thrumming along beautifully, and the crowd went wild, singing and dancing. The end of the song approached, and I couldn't remember how it ended, but oh well—we'd nailed it at sound check, I'd follow the cues. But I missed the cues. The song came to a resounding conclusion. Except . . . I kept playing. Just me. And so I ended my career like I started it: out of my depth and with my ass hanging out.

*

I HAVE TO believe that there was a subliminal motivator for my continuing to play that night. Some part of me wasn't ready to stop.

*

ON THE OTHER hand, I was beyond ready to be done, already checking out, stepping into the future. Maybe that's why I missed the ending. I was already gone.

*

I SAID THIS before: I blow endings all the time. During one gig, filling in for the drummer of a band I loved, I asked the singer how we were going to end a song that faded out on the record. *We'll just end it*, he said. *We'll feel it*. But I've never had a good feel for endings. Not on drums. Not in writing. Not in life. Is this the best I can do? Either clamp down and control it, or let it disintegrate? Maybe working harder as a writer will give me a chance to finally learn how to listen, to feel my way to an elegant and timely ending. Maybe I'll develop those chops on my new instrument, the Precise V5 Rolling Ball pen.

*

THERE ARE ONLY a few movies with truly perfect endings: *The Bad News Bears* is one.

It refuses to wrap every narrative thread, dropping entirely a subplot about Coach Buttermaker's romantic past with young pitcher Amanda Whurlitzer's mother. Each character emerges transformed in some way—they've learned to collaborate, to defend one another, to push themselves harder for a shared purpose; they've become less selfish, less cynical, and in the specific case of Coach Buttermaker, a little less drunk. All without losing the spark of their imperfect, idiosyncratic selves. I'd like the ending of this story to resemble theirs. I've changed and not changed. Tonight I'll go to bed with my cannabis gummy, and I'll continue to do so until I figure out a better way. My macrobiotic teacher Michio Kushi writes that our cells, tissues, skin, and organs are continuously recreated, that even our consciousness is constantly evolving. Yes. And. We tend to rebuild in similar, recognizable patterns.

In a beautiful fuck-you to the standard underdog sports team narrative, the Bears lose the big game in the end. It's not sad, because we see that they have won more than they've lost. If this here was a standard, predictable story, I would have nailed the ending to that ELO song.

But you can't quit being yourself.

Acknowledgments

I DON'T KNOW how to adequately express my appreciation to Maryse Meijer for asking the perfect questions and making all the right changes and suggestions, helping me to transform a thin and jumbled first draft into the book I wanted to write. May all writers be blessed with such a generous, intelligent, and empathetic editor and friend. Much gratitude to everyone at Agate, especially Doug Seibold for giving me the opportunity to write and publish another quirky, unconventional book and Amanda Gibson for understanding IQE from the start, keeping the editorial process painlessly on track, and inspiring me to make the book clearer, more substantive, more accurate, and so much better. Thanks are also due to production manager Jane Seibold and publicity manager Jaqueline Jarik. I'm lucky to have a wonderful agent, Jenni Ferrari-Adler at Union Literary. Many conversations with friends fed this book but special props to Suzanne Clores and Kurt Riemersma for inspiring talks about pot-smoking in movies and Biden-era headlines; to Dag Juhlin for sharing my admiration for the drunken

Replacements; to Catherine Carrigan and Daniel Immerwahr for the inside scoop on bar mitzvah candy; to Nora O'Connor for talking with me about booze-free living and for loaning me *Quit Like a Woman*; to Janas Hoyt for The Twinkie Theory; to Paul Strohm for his decades-ago observations about "Changed the Locks"; and to Becca Dudley for brilliant brainstorming on how to end a book about quitting. Thank you to my friend and drumming mentor Gerald Dowd for inviting me to read an early draft of the social media chapter at Fitzgerald's; and to my fellow Sunshine Boy Jacqueline Schimmel for steadfast support. Big love and grateful hugs to my whole family, especially my mother, Carol, and father, Don, my amazing children—Henry, Jonah, my future daughter-in-law Cecilia—and to my husband, Jake: an interested and encouraging reader who suggested many useful sources, especially the work of Gregory Bateson. You are my difference that makes a difference.

Notes

1   Michael S. Pollard, Joan S. Tucker, Harold D. Green, "Changes in Adult Alcohol Use and Consequences During the COVID-19 Pandemic in the US," *JAMA Network Open* 3, no. 9 (September 2020), https://doi.org/10.1001/jamanetworkopen.2020.22942.

2   Kate Julian, "America Has a Drinking Problem," *The Atlantic*, July/August 2021, https://www.theatlantic.com/magazine/archive/2021/07/america-drinking-alone-problem/619017/.

3   Sam Binkley, *Getting Loose: Lifestyle Consumption in the 1970s* (Durham: Duke University Press, 2007), 3.

4   Binkley, 9.

5   Binkley, 3.

6   Julian.

7   Jonathan Koppel, David C. Rubin, "Recent Advances in Understanding the Reminiscence Bump: The Importance of Cues in Guiding Recall from Autobiographical Memory," *Current Directions in Psychological Science* 25, no. 2 (April 2016): 135–49, https://doi.org/10.1177/0963721416631955.

8   Victor C. Strasburger, Barbara J. Wilson, Amy B. Jordan, *Children, Adolescents, and the Media*, 3rd ed. (Thousand Oaks: Sage, 2013), 515.

9   Buddhism Stack Exchange, "Asubha Practice," January 18, 2017, https://buddhism.stackexchange.com/questions/19000/asubha-practice.

10 Gregory Bateson, "The Cybernetics of 'Self': A Theory of Alcoholism." *Psychiatry* 24, no. 2 (February 1971): 11.

11   Michio Kushi, *The Cancer Prevention Diet* (New York: St Martin's Press, 1983), 23.

12   Bateson, 9.

13   Ann Lee, "Stop Talking About 'Wine O'Clock': Holly Whitaker on How Women Can Stop Drinking – And Get Happy," *The Guardian*, last modified January 14, 2020, https://www.theguardian.com/lifeandstyle/2020/jan/14/aas-rules-are-for-men-holly-whitaker-on-how-women-can-stop-drinking-and-get-happy.

14   Holly Whitaker, *Quit Like a Woman: The Radical Choice to Not Drink in a Culture Obsessed with Alcohol* (New York: Dial Press, 2019), 26.

15   Whitaker, 31–35.

16   Whitaker, 79.

17   Whitaker, 92.

18   Whitaker, 135.

19   Whitaker, 104.

20   Edward Slingerland, *Drunk: How We Sipped, Danced, and Stumbled Our Way to Civilization* (New York: Little, Brown Spark, 2021), 8.

21   Slingerland, 15.

22   Slingerland, 12.

23   Slingerland, 104.

24   Slingerland, 105

25   Leo Tolstoy, *Recollections and Essays* (London: Oxford University Press, 1961), 71.

26   Slingerland, 116.

27   Proverbs 31:6.

28   Aldous Huxley, *The Doors of Perception* (London: Chatto & Windus, 1954; New York: HarperCollins, 2009), 62.

29   Slingerland, 204.

30   Slingerland, 204.

31   Slingerland, 215.

32   Andrew Weil, *The Natural Mind* (1972; rev., Boston/New York: Houghton Mifflin, 2004), xiii.

33   Bateson, 16.

34   Bateson, 16.

35 William Dufty, *Sugar Blues* (New York: Hachette, 1975), 12.

36 For more details about this history and research, see Gary Taubes, *The Case Against Sugar* (New York: Anchor Books, 2016).

37 Taubes, 41.

38 Daniel P. Finney, "Creators Are Clear: 'Pufnstuf' Was Definitely an Acid Trip," *St. Louis Post-Dispatch*, February 17, 2004, D3.

39 Sarah Jio, "You Won't Believe the 1960s Ad for Sugar," *Glamour*, December 7, 2009, https://www.glamour.com/story/you-wont-believe-this-hilariou-1.

40 Marissa Higgins, "Where Does 'Honeymoon' Come From, Anyway?" *Bustle*, January 28, 2016, https://www.bustle.com/articles/138267-where-does-the-word-honeymoon-come-from-heres-a-look-at-the-history-of-both-the.

41 Twinkies were originally going to be called "Little Shortcake Fingers," which maybe I'm just thinking too much about sex now but also sounds vaguely dirty?

42 *Encyclopedia Britannica*, s.v. "deva," March 9, 2015, https://www.britannica.com/topic/deva-religious-being.

43 Thea Summer Deer, "Who Are the Plant Devas," *Wisdom of the Plant Devas*, https://wisdomoftheplantdevas.com/book/who-are-the-plant-devas/. For more, see Deer's book: *The Wisdom of the Plant Devas* (Rochester: Bear & Company, 2011).

44 Susan Raatz, "The Question of Sugar," *USDA Agricultural Research Service*, last modified July 24, 2019, https://www.ars.usda.gov/plains-area/gfnd/gfhnrc/docs/news-2012/the-question-of-sugar/.

45 Patanjali, *The Yoga Sutra*, trans. Barbara Stoler Miller as *Yoga: Discipline of Freedom* (Berkeley: University of California Press, 1995), 56.

46 Not to be mistaken for the Twinkie Defense: "The term 'Twinkie defense' is an umbrella term that, in the most general sense, refers to an unconventional defensive argument. The term originated from the 1979 trial of Dan White, a San Francisco politician, who was charged with first-degree murder [including the murder of Harvey Milk]. A testifying psychiatrist pointed out that White's consumption

of sugary foods, such as Twinkies, could lead to diminished capacity." From the Cornell Law School Legal Information Institute, https://www.law.cornell.edu/wex/twinkie_defense.

47   Dufty, 218.

48   Bonni Goldstein, *Cannabis Is Medicine: How Medical Cannabis and CBD Are Healing Everything from Anxiety to Chronic Pain* (New York: Little, Brown Spark, 2020), 30.

49   Goldstein, 38.

50   Goldstein, 31.

51   Michael Pollan, *The Botany of Desire: A Plant's-Eye View of the World* (New York: Random House, 2002), 116.

52   Pollan, 162.

53   Pollan, 161.

54   Pollan, 168.

55   Pollan, 162.

56   Pollan, 162.

57   Pollan, 168.

58   Pollan, 162.

59   William Blake, "Auguries of Innocence," in *Blake's Poetry and Designs*, ed. Mary Lynn Johnson and John E. Grant (New York: W. W. Norton, 2008), 403.

60   See Erica Jong's *Fear of Flying* (1973). Jong coined the concept of "the zipless fuck," sex with no strings attached.

61   Randi Melissa Schuster, Jodi Gilman, David Schoenfeld, John Evenden, Maya Hareli, Christine Ulysse, Emily Nip, Ailish Hanly, Haiyue Zhang, A. Eden Evins, "One Month of Cannabis Abstinence in Adolescents and Young Adults Is Associated with Improved Memory," *Journal of Clinical Psychiatry* 76, no. 2 (October 2018): 17m11977, https://doi.org/10.4088/JCP.17m11977.

62   The 1997 film *The Ice Storm,* directed by Ang Lee, takes a dark look at the pathos of the '70s and the catastrophic potential of parental self-absorption and negligence.

63   Flowhub, "Cannabis Industry Statistics 2022: How the Industry Is Performing and Where It's Heading," accessed December 16, 2022,

https://flowhub.com/cannabis-industry-statistics.

64   Ted Van Green, "Americans Overwhelmingly Say Marijuana
       Should Be Legal for Medical or Recreational Use," *Pew Research
       Center*, November 22, 2022, https://www.pewresearch.org/fact-
       tank/2022/11/22/americans-overwhelmingly-say-marijuana-should-
       be-legal-for-medical-or-recreational-use/.

65   Flowhub.

66   Ben Blanchett, "Tucker Carlson Points Finger at Women and Weed
       for Latest Mass Shooting," *Yahoo Finance*, July 5, 2022, https://finance.
       yahoo.com/news/tucker-carlson-points-finger-women-045131296.
       html.

67   Thomas Schierenbeck, Dieter Riemann, Mathias Berger, Magdolna
       Hornyak, "Effect of Illicit Recreational Drugs upon Sleep: Cocaine,
       Ecstasy and Marijuana," *Sleep Medicine Reviews* 12, no. 5 (October
       2008): 381–9, https://doi.org/10.1016/j.smrv.2007.12.004.

68   Pollan, *The Botany of Desire*, 178.

69   Pollan, 178.

70   Jann Gumbiner, "History of Cannabis in India," *Psychology Today*,
       June 16, 2011, https://www.psychologytoday.com/us/blog/the-
       teenage-mind/201106/history-cannabis-in-india.

71   Stephan Pretorius, "The Significance of the Use of Ganja as a
       Religious Ritual in the Rastafari Movement," *Verbum et Ecclesia* 27, no.
       3 (September 2006): 1012–30.

72   Marc-Antoine Crocq, "History of Cannabis and the
       Endocannabinoid System," *Dialogues in Clinical Neuroscience* 22, no. 3
       (September 2020): 223–28, https://doi.org/10.31887/DCNS.2020.22.3/
       mcrocq.

73   Vance Mariner, "Retroanalysis: The Coffee Achievers," *The Marketing
       Smart Aleck*, June 9, 2014, https://marketingsmartaleck.wordpress.
       com/2014/06/09/retroanalysis-the-coffee-achievers/.

74   For more on caffeine (and for the source of these caffeine statistics)
       see Michael Pollan, *This Is Your Mind on Plants* (New York: Penguin,
       2021).

75   Pollan, *This Is Your Mind on Plants*, 116.

76   Chris Nash, response to "Why do Mormons not drink tea or coffee?" *Quora*, accessed October 23, 2022, https://www.quora.com/Why-do-Mormons-not-drink-tea-or-coffee.

77   Slingerland, 57.

78   Pollan, *This Is Your Mind on Plants*, 122–23.

79   Pollan, 111.

80   "Sophrosyne," The Theoi Project, accessed October 23, 2022, https://www.theoi.com/Daimon/Sophrosyne.html.

81   Anne-Laure Le Cunff, "Sophrosyne: The Art of Mindful Moderation," *Ness Labs*, accessed October 23, 2022, https://nesslabs.com/sophrosyne.

82   Veronica Barassi, *Child Data Citizen: How Tech Companies Are Profiling Us from Before Birth* (Cambridge: MIT Press, 2020), 25.

83   Gary W. Small, Jooyeon Lee, Aaron Kaufman, Jason Jalil, Prabha Siddarth, Himaja Gaddipati, Teena D. Moody, Susan Bookheimer, "Brain Health Consequences of Digital Technology Use," *Dialogues in Clinical Neuroscience* 22, no. 2 (2020): 180–82.

84   Harvard professor emerita Shoshana Zuboff coined the term "surveillance capitalism," and she defines it as "the unilateral claiming of private human experience as free raw material for translation into behavioral data. These data are then computed and packaged as prediction products and sold into behavioral futures markets—business customers with a commercial interest in knowing what we will do now, soon, and later." John Laider, "High Tech Is Watching You," *The Harvard Gazette*, March 4, 2019, https://news.harvard.edu/gazette/story/2019/03/harvard-professor-says-surveillance-capitalism-is-undermining-democracy/.

85   Pema Chödrön, *How We Live Is How We Die* (Boulder: Shambhala, 2022), 15.

86   Koun Franz, "Buddhism's 'Five Remembrances' Are Wake-Up Calls for Us All," *Lion's Roar*, March 30, 2021, https://www.lionsroar.com/buddhisms-five-remembrances-are-wake-up-calls-for-us-all/.

87   R. E. Menzies, L. F. Whittle, "Stoicism and Death Acceptance: Integrating Stoic Philosophy in Cognitive Behaviour Therapy for

Death Anxiety," *Discover Psychology* 2, no. 11 (2022), https://doi.
org/10.1007/s44202-022-00023-9.

88   John 15:19.

89   John 17:14.

90   Carl L. Hart, *Drug Use for Grown-Ups: Chasing Liberty in the Land of Fear*
      (New York: Penguin, 2021), 177.

91   Hart, 11.

92   Gregory Bateson, *A Sacred Unity: Further Steps to an Ecology of Mind*
      (New York: HarperCollins, 1991), 211–12.

93   Charles Bukowski, *Reach for the Sun, Vol. 3: Charles Bukowski's Selected
      Letters* (New York: HarperCollins e-books, 2009), 77–79.

94   Eula Biss, *Having and Being Had* (New York: Riverhead, 2020), 236.

95   Biss, 166.

96   Noreen Malone, "The Age of Anti-Ambition," *New York Times Magazine*,
      February 20, 2022.

97   Jean Bolen, *Goddesses in Older Women: Archetypes in Women Over Fifty*
      (New York: HarperCollins, 2014), 31.

98   Members and special guests of BOTO include: Gail Greenwood,
      Jen Trynin, Magen Tracy, Hilken Mancini, Chris Toppn, Tamora
      Gooding, Kameelah Benjamin-Fuller, Melissa Gibbs, Michelle
      Paulhus, Jen D'Angora, Cherry Currie, Debbi Peterson, Nora
      O'Connor, Jennifer Hall, Amy Griffin, Kelly Hogan, Kate Tucker,
      Kimi Hayes, Sadie DuPuis, Gracie Deneen, and Kate Piccan. YOU
      ALL ROCK.

About the Author

Freda Love Smith is a writer, teacher, and retired indie rock drummer. Her first book, *Red Velvet Underground: A Rock Memoir, with Recipes*, was published in 2015. She teaches at Northwestern University, Lesley University, and Bookends & Beginnings, and she played drums with Blake Babies, Antenna, Mysteries of Life, Gentleman Caller, Some Girls, and Sunshine Boys. She lives in Evanston, Illinois, with her husband.